CAMBRIDGE LIBRARY COLLECTION

Books of enduring scholarly value

English Men of Letters

In the 1870s, Macmillan publishers began to issue a series of books called 'English Men of Letters' – biographies of English writers by other English writers. The general editor of the series was the journalist, critic, politician, and supporter (and later biographer) of Gladstone, John Morley (1838–1923). The aim was to provide a short introduction to each subject and his works, but also that the life should illuminate the works, and vice versa. The subjects range chronologically from Chaucer to Thackeray and Dickens, and an important feature of the series is that many of the authors (Henry James on Hawthorne, Ward on Dickens) were discussing writers of the previous generation, and some (Trollope on Thackeray) had even known their subjects personally. The series exemplifies the British approach to literary biography and criticism at the end of the nineteenth century, and also reveals which authors were at that time regarded as canonical.

Locke

This biography of the philosopher John Locke (1632–1704) was published in the first series of English Men of Letters in 1880. Its author, Thomas Fowler (1832–1904) held the posts of Wykeham Professor of Logic, President of Corpus Christi College, and Vice-Chancellor of Oxford University; the editor of the series, John Morley, had been his pupil. The influence of Locke is pervasive in many fields – theology, education, psychology, economics and political theory as well as philosophy – and Fowler analyses the effect of his writings in five chapters (one dedicated to the *Essay Concerning Human Understanding*) as well as giving a chronological account of Locke's life from his obscure beginnings through his time at Oxford, his role in the household of the earl of Shaftesbury, and his two periods of travel in Europe, to a position at the heart of political and intellectual life in Restoration England.

T0370829

Cambridge University Press has long been a pioneer in the reissuing of out-of-print titles from its own backlist, producing digital reprints of books that are still sought after by scholars and students but could not be reprinted economically using traditional technology. The Cambridge Library Collection extends this activity to a wider range of books which are still of importance to researchers and professionals, either for the source material they contain, or as landmarks in the history of their academic discipline.

Drawing from the world-renowned collections in the Cambridge University Library, and guided by the advice of experts in each subject area, Cambridge University Press is using state-of-the-art scanning machines in its own Printing House to capture the content of each book selected for inclusion. The files are processed to give a consistently clear, crisp image, and the books finished to the high quality standard for which the Press is recognised around the world. The latest print-on-demand technology ensures that the books will remain available indefinitely, and that orders for single or multiple copies can quickly be supplied.

The Cambridge Library Collection will bring back to life books of enduring scholarly value (including out-of-copyright works originally issued by other publishers) across a wide range of disciplines in the humanities and social sciences and in science and technology.

Locke

THOMAS FOWLER

CAMBRIDGE UNIVERSITY PRESS

Cambridge, New York, Melbourne, Madrid, Cape Town,
Singapore, São Paolo, Delhi, Tokyo, Mexico City

Published in the United States of America by Cambridge University Press, New York

www.cambridge.org
Information on this title: www.cambridge.org/9781108034562

© in this compilation Cambridge University Press 2011

This edition first published 1880
This digitally printed version 2011

ISBN 978-1-108-03456-2 Paperback

English Men of Letters

EDITED BY JOHN MORLEY

LOCKE

LOCKE

BY

THOMAS FOWLER

PROFESSOR OF LOGIC IN THE UNIVERSITY OF OXFORD.

London:

MACMILLAN AND CO.

1880.

The Right of Translation and Reproduction is Reserved.

NOTE.

In writing the chapters on Locke's Life, I have derived much information from the biographies of Lord King and Mr. Fox Bourne, especially from the latter, which contains a large amount of most interesting documents never before printed. In a work like the present, where numerous foot-notes would be out of place, I am obliged to content myself with this general acknowledgment. I may add that I have also referred to several other authorities, both printed and in manuscript; and, in some cases, I believe that my account will be found more precise than that given in the larger biographies.

CONTENTS.

LOCKE.

CHAPTER I.

JOHN LOCKE, perhaps the greatest, but certainly the most characteristic, of English philosophers, was born at Wrington, a pleasant village in the north of Somersetshire, August 29, 1632. His family, however, resided in the village of Pensford, and the parish of Publow, within a few miles of Bristol. It was there, probably, that Locke spent the greater part of his early life. His mother appears to have died while he was young. From his father, John Locke (b. 1606), who seems to have inherited a fair estate, and who practised, with some success, as a country attorney, he probably derived, if not his earliest instruction, at least some of his earliest influences and some of his most sterling characteristics. "From Mr. Locke I have often heard of his father," says Lady Masham in a MS. letter quoted by Mr. Fox-Bourne in his Life of Locke, "that he was a man of parts. Mr. Locke never mentioned him but with great respect and affection. His father used a conduct towards him when young that he often spoke of afterwards with great approbation. It

B

was the being severe to him by keeping him in much awe, and at a distance, when he was a boy, but relaxing, still by degrees, of that severity as he grew up to be a man, till, he being become capable of it, he lived perfectly with him as a friend. And I remember he has told me that his father, after he was a man, solemnly asked his pardon for having struck him once in a passion when he was a boy."

Locke's boyhood coincided pretty nearly with the troubles of the Civil Wars. "I no sooner perceived myself in the world," he wrote in 1660, " but I found myself in a storm which has lasted almost hitherto." His father, when Locke was hardly ten years old, publicly announced, in the parish church of Publow, his assent to the protest of the Long Parliament, and, a few weeks afterwards, took the field, on the Parliamentary side, as captain of a troop of horse in a regiment of volunteers. Though the fortunes of the family undoubtedly suffered from this step on the part of the young attorney, the political and religious interests which it created and kept alive in his household must have contributed, in no small degree, to shape the character and determine the sympathies of his elder son.

Locke, then, may be regarded as having been fortunate in his early surroundings. Born in one of the more charming of the rural districts of England, not far, however, from a city which was then one of the most important centres of commerce and politics; sprung from respectable and well-to-do parents, of whom the father, at least, possessed more than ordinary intelligence; accustomed, from his earliest boyhood, to watch the progress of great events, and to listen to the discussion of great and stirring questions : there seems to have been nothing in

his early life to retard or mar the development of his
genius, and much that we may not unreasonably connect
with the marked peculiarities, both moral and intellectual,
of his subsequent career.

It was probably in the year 1646 that, through the
interest of Colonel Popham, a friend and client of his
father, Locke was admitted at Westminster School, where,
probably in the following year, he was elected on the
foundation.   Here he must have remained about six
years, till his election to a Westminster Studentship at
Christ Church, Oxford, in 1652. Of the manner in which
Locke spent these years we have no definite information.
The stern disciplinarian, Dr. Busby, had been head master
for about eight years when he entered the school, and
among his schoolfellows, senior to him by about a year,
were Dryden and South.   The friends whom he made at
Westminster, though highly respectable in after-life, did
not achieve any great reputation.   Of the studies which
then constituted the ordinary school curriculum, his
matured opinions are to be found in the " Thoughts concerning Education," which will be described in a subsequent chapter.   To judge from this book, the impressions
left on Locke's mind by our English public school education were not of a pleasant or favourable kind.

Locke appears to have commenced his residence at
Christ Church in the Michaelmas Term of 1652, soon
after he had turned twenty years of age.   His matricu-
lation before the Vice-Chancellor bears date Nov. 27.
Since the outbreak of the Civil Wars, both the University
and the College had undergone many vicissitudes.   At
the moment when Locke entered, Cromwell was Chancellor, and Dr. John Owen, who was destined to be for
some time the leading resident, had been recently ap-

pointed Dean of Christ Church and Vice-Chancellor of the
University.   Owen was an Independent, and, for a divine
of that age, a man of remarkably tolerant and liberal views.
Though, then as now, a dignitary in Owen's position
probably had and could have but little intercourse with the
junior members of his society, it is not improbable that
Locke may have derived his first bias towards those
opinions on the question of religious toleration, for which
he afterwards became so famous, from the publications
and the practice of the puritan Dean of Christ Church.
Locke's tutor was a Mr. Cole, afterwards Principal of St.
Mary Hall, but of his relations with his pupil we hear
nothing of any importance.   Wood calls him a " fanatical
tutor," by which, of course, he does not mean more than
that he was a puritan.

During the Civil Wars, the discipline and reputation
of the Universities, however we may apportion the blame,
seem to have suffered most severely.   In these troublous
times, indeed, it could hardly be otherwise   There is considerable evidence to show that, in the Little or Barbone's
Parliament of 1653, there was a serious attempt to suppress the Colleges and Universities altogether, and to apply
the proceeds of their estates, as Clarendon tells us, " for
the public service, and to ease the people from the payment of taxes and contributions."   If such an attempt
ever had any chance of success — and from an ora-
tion of Dr. Owen we may infer that it had—it must
have spread consternation amongst University circles,
and been a frequent subject of conversation during the
early period of Locke's residence in Oxford.   But the
Puritan party, which was now in the ascendant, was
determined that, at any rate, no handle should be given
to the enemy by any lack of discipline or by the infre-

quency of religious exercises. "Frequent preaching in every house," Anthony à Wood tells us, "was the chief matter aimed at" by the Visitors appointed by Cromwell in 1652. Thus, on June 27, 1653, they ordered that "all Bachelors of Arts and Undergraduates in Colleges and Halls be required, every Lord's day, to give an account to some person of known ability and piety of the sermons they had heard and their attendance on other religious exercises that day. The Heads also or Deputies of the said Societies, with all above the Degree of Bachelor, were then ordered to be personally present at the performance of the said exercise, and to take care that it be attended with prayer and such other duties of religion as are proper to such a meeting." In addition to the Sunday observances, there were also, in most Colleges, if not in all, one or two sermons or religious meetings in the course of the week. Locke, if we may judge from his character in later years, must have occasionally found these tedious, and doubtless lengthy, exercises somewhat irksome and unprofitable. But we do not meet in his writings with any definite complaints of them, as we do of the scholastic disputations and some other parts of the academical course as pursued at that time. Of the disputations, which then constituted a very important element in the University curriculum, he expresses an unfavourable, perhaps too unfavourable an opinion. Writing in 1690, in the "Thoughts concerning Education," he says: "If the use and end of right reasoning be to have right notions and a right judgment of things, to distinguish between truth and falsehood, right and wrong, and to act accordingly, be sure not to let your son be bred up in the art and formality of disputing— either practising it himself or admiring it in others — unless, instead of an able man, you desire to have him an insig-

nificant wrangler, opiniater in discourse, and priding
himself in contradicting others ; or, which is worse, questioning everything, and thinking there is no such thing
as truth to be sought, but only victory, in disputing.
There cannot be anything so disingenuous, so unbecoming
a gentleman, or any one who pretends to be a rational
creature, as not to yield to plain reason and the conviction
of clear arguments. Is there anything more inconsistent
with civil conversation and the end of all debate, than
not to take an answer, though ever so full and satisfactory ? . . . . For this, in short, is the way and perfection
of logical disputes, that the opponent never takes any
answer, nor the respondent ever yields to any argument."
With the logic and rhetoric, the Latin speaking and Latin
writing, then in vogue, Locke is almost equally discontented. In fact, he looked back, in after-life, with little
gratitude on the somewhat dry course of studies which
the University then prescribed to its younger scholars. " I
have often heard him say, in reference to his first years
spent in the University," says Lady Masham, "that he
had so small satisfaction there from his studies, as finding
very little light brought thereby to his understanding,
that he became discontented with his manner of life, and
wished his father had rather designed him for anything
else than what he was destined to, apprehending that his
no greater progress in knowledge proceeded from his not
being fitted or capacitated to be a scholar." We must,
however, by no means infer that Locke had not derived
considerable benefit from the discipline which he dis-
parages. At any rate, the scholastic teaching of Oxford
had a large share in forming, by reaction, many of his
most characteristic opinions, while the Essay, in almost
every page, bears distinctive marks of his early studies.

Notwithstanding his depreciation, amounting often to ridicule, of the subjects he had learnt in his youth, we can hardly doubt that, if Locke had been brought up in an University where logic and philosophy did not form part of the course, his greatest work would never have been written.

Mr. Fox-Bourne attempts to supply a detailed account of the lectures which Locke attended, and the course of studies which he pursued, during his undergraduate and bachelor days. This account, however, betrays an innocent belief in the rigid enforcement and observance of University and College statutes which, I am sorry to say, I cannot share. Minute regulations regarding courses of study and attendance at lectures are apt very soon to fall into desuetude, and it is impossible now to reconstruct with any accuracy, from the perusal of merely formal documents, a plan of the student life of the Commonwealth. It is to be much regretted that Locke and his contemporaries have not left us more specific information on the subject. All we can now say is that, if the authorities duly enforced their statutes and regulations, especially those relating to professorial lectures, many of which were appointed to be given at eight o'clock in the morning, the students of those days had by no means an easier time of it than their successors, even in these days of competition and examinations.

The stated regulations and prescribed statutes of a seat of learning have, however, often far less to do with the formation of a student's mind than the society of the young men of his own age with whom his residence throws him into contact. Young men often educate one another far more effectually than they can be educated by their tutors or their books. The mutual confidences, the lively

interchange of repartee, the free discussion of all manner
of subjects in college rooms or during the afternoon walk,
are often far more stimulating and informing to the intellect than the professorial lecture, however learned, or the
tutorial catechizing, however searching. Of this less formal
and more agreeable species of education Locke appears to
have enjoyed his full share. He was not, according to
the account which he gave of himself to Lady Masham,
"any very hard student," but "sought the company of
pleasant and witty men, with whom he likewise took
great delight in corresponding by letters; and in conversation and these correspondences he spent for some years
much of his time."

It should be noticed that in the year 1654 Owen published a volume of congratulatory verses addressed to
Cromwell on the treaty recently concluded with the
Dutch, entitled " Musarum Oxoniensium ἐλαιοφορία."
Among the many contributors to this volume, young and
old, was Locke, who wrote a short copy of Latin, and a
longer copy of English verses. These compositions do
not rise much above, or sink much below, the ordinary
level of such exercises; but what is curious is that Locke's
first published efforts in literature should have been in
verse, especially when we bear in mind his strong and
somewhat perverse judgment on verse-writing in § 174
of the " Thoughts concerning Education." The fact of
his having been invited to contribute to the volume shows
that he was regarded as one of the more promising young
students of his time.

To the period of Locke's life covered by this chapter
probably belong some interesting notes on philosophy and
its divisions, found in his father's memorandum-book.
These reflections afford evidence that he had already

begun to think for himself, independently of the scholastic
traditions. I append one or two characteristic extracts :—

"Dialectic, that is Logic, is to make reasons to grow, and
improve both Physic and also Ethic, which is Moral Philosophy."

"Moral Philosophy is the knowledge of precepts of all honest
manners which reason acknowledgeth to belong and appertain
to man's nature, as the things in which we differ from beasts.
It is also necessary for the comely government of man's life."

"Necessity was the first finder-out of moral philosophy, and
experience (which is a trusty teacher) was the first master
thereof."

Locke took his B.A. degree on the 14th of February,
1655-6, and his M.A. degree on the 29th of June,
1658, the latter on the same day with Nathaniel Crewe,
afterwards Lord Crewe, Bishop of Durham, and Joseph
Glanvill, the celebrated writer on witchcraft, and author
of *Scepsis Scientifica.* The statutable time of taking
both degrees was anticipated, but irregularities of this kind
were not then infrequent. On the 24th of December,
1660, he was appointed Greek Lecturer at Christ Church
for the ensuing year, thus taking his place among the
authorized teachers of his college, and so entering on a
new phase of university life. Very shortly after this
date, namely, on Feb. 13, 1660-1, the elder Locke died, æt.
fifty-four. Locke's only brother, Thomas, who was some
years younger than himself, died of consumption shortly
after his father. By the time, therefore, that Locke had
fairly entered on his duties as an officer of his college, he
was left alone of all his family.

Though it was not till a much later period of his life that
Locke published any works, his pen was at this time by

no means idle. In 1661 he began a series of common-
place books, often containing long articles on the subjects
which were occupying his thoughts at the time. It is,
moreover, to the period immediately preceding or immediately following the Restoration, that Mr. Fox-Bourne
attributes an unpublished and till recently unknown
Essay, entitled, " Reflections upon the Roman Commonwealth." Many of the remarks in this Essay already
show what we should call liberal opinions in religion and
politics, and anticipate views long afterwards propounded
in the works on government and toleration. The religion
instituted by Numa is idealized, as having insisted on
only two articles of faith, the goodness of the gods, and
the necessity of worshipping them, " in which worship
the chief of all was to be innocent, good, and just."
Thus it avoided " creating heresies and schisms," and
" narrowing the bottom of religion by clogging it with
creeds and catechisms and endless niceties about the
essences, properties, and attributes of God."

Of more interest, perhaps, is another unpublished
treatise, written just after the Restoration, in which
Locke asks, and answers in the affirmative, the following
question : Whether the civil magistrate may lawfully im-
pose and determine the use of indifferent things in reference to religious worship. This tract seems to have been
intended as a remonstrance with those of the author's own
party who questioned any right in the civil magistrate to
interfere in religious matters, and who, therefore, were
ready to reject with disdain the assurances of compromise
and moderation contained in the king's declaration on
ecclesiastical affairs, issued at the beginning of his reign.
Locke, at that time, like many other moderate men, seems
to have entertained the most sanguine hopes of pacification

and good government under the rule of the new monarch.
" As for myself," he writes, " there is no one can have a
greater respect and veneration for authority than I.   I no
sooner perceived myself in the world, but I found myself
in a storm, which has lasted almost hitherto, and therefore
cannot but entertain the approaches of a calm with the
greatest joy and satisfaction."   "I find that a general
freedom is but a general bondage, that the popular as-
serters of public liberty are the greatest ingrossers of it
too, and not unfitly called its keepers."   This reaction,
however, against the past, and these sanguine expecta-
tions of the future, can have lasted but a short time.   The
tendencies of the new government were soon apparent,
and the pamphlet was never published.

CHAPTER II.

LOCKE, at the time of his father's death and his entrance
on college office, was in his twenty-ninth year. At the
election of college officers on Christmas Eve, 1662, he was
transferred from the Greek Lectureship to the Lectureship
in Rhetoric, and, on the 23rd of December in the following year, he was again transferred to another office. This
office was the Censorship of Moral Philosophy (the Senior
Censorship); the Censorship of Natural Philosophy (the
Junior Censorship) he appears never to have held. On
the 23rd of December, 1665, he is no longer in office,
being now merely one of the twenty senior M.A. students,
called "Theologi," who were bound to be in priests'
orders. Of the manner in which Locke discharged his
duties as a lecturer we have no record. He seems also
to have served in the capacity of tutor to several undergraduates at this period, but of his relations to his pupils
we, unfortunately, know next to nothing.

How is it that Locke, holding a clerical studentship,
was not a clergyman? The disturbed condition of the
Church and the Universities during the last quarter of a
century had probably led to great laxity in the enforcement
of college statutes and by-laws. Moreover, for a time it

would seem, he seriously contemplated taking the step of
entering holy orders, and the authorities of his college
would probably be unwilling to force upon him a hasty
decision.   At length, however, he finally abandoned this
idea, deciding in favour of the profession of physic.   In
the ordinary course he would have forfeited his studentship, but he was fortunate to obtain a royal dispensation
(by no means an uncommon mode of intervention at that
time), retaining him in his place, " that he may still have
further time to prosecute his studies."   This dispensation
is dated Nov. 14, 1666.

Meanwhile, Locke had paid his first visit to the Continent.   The occasion of it was an embassy to the Elector
of Brandenburg, whose alliance or neutrality it was sought
to obtain in the then pending war with Holland.   Sir
Walter Vane was head of the embassy, and Locke, who
probably owed his nomination to the interest of his old
schoolfellow, William Godolphin, was appointed secretary.
They left England in the middle of November, 1665, and
arrived at Cleve, the capital of Brandenburg, on the 30th
of the same month (Dec. 9, N.S.).   Here they remained
for two months, the mission coming to nothing, in consequence of the English Government being unable or unwilling to advance the money which the Elector required
as the price of his adhesion.   The state-papers addressed
by the Ambassador to the Government at home are mainly
in Locke's handwriting, but far more interesting than
these are the private letters addressed by Locke to his
friends, Mr. Strachey, of Sutton Court, near Bristol, and
the celebrated Robert Boyle.   These are full of graphic
touches descriptive of the manners and peculiarities of the
people among whom he found himself.   Like a conscientious sight-seer, he availed himself of the various

opportunities of observing their eating and drinking, attended their devotions, whether Catholic, Calvinist, or Lutheran, submitted himself to be bored by poetasters and sucking theologians, and consoled himself for the difficulty of finding a pair of gloves by noting the tardiness of German commerce. Though he had "thought for a while to take leave of all University affairs," he found himself ridden pitilessly by an "academic goblin."

"I no sooner was got here, but I was welcomed with a divinity disputation. I was no sooner rid of that, but I found myself up to the ears in poetry, and overwhelmed in Helicon." "But my University goblin left me not so; for the next day, when I thought I had been rode out only to airing, I was had to a foddering of chopped hay or logic forsooth! Poor *materia prima* was canvassed cruelly, stripped of all the gay dress of her forms, and shown naked to us, though, I must confess, I had not eyes good enough to see her. The young monks (which one would not guess by their looks) are subtle people, and dispute as eagerly for *materia prima* as if they were to make their dinner on it, and, perhaps, sometimes it is all their meal, for which others' charity is more to be blamed than their stomachs. . . . The truth is, here hog-shearing is much in its glory, and our disputing in Oxford comes as far short of it as the rhetoric of Carfax does that of Billingsgate."

At a dinner, described with a good deal of humour, with the Franciscan friars, he was still pursued by his Oxford recollections :—

"The prior was a good plump fellow, that had more belly than brains; and methought was very fit to be reverenced, and not much unlike some head of a college."

One circumstance Locke noticed much to the advantage of the foreigners, namely, their good-natured toleration for each other's opinions. Writing to Boyle, he says,—

" The distance in their churches gets not into their houses.
They quietly permit one another to choose their way to heaven ;
for I cannot observe any quarrels or animosities amongst them
upon the account of religion.   This good correspondence is
owing partly to the power of the magistrate, and partly to the
prudence and good nature of the people, who, as I find by inquiring, entertain different opinions without any secret hatred
or rancour."

And though, like most Englishmen, of decided Protestant convictions, travelling on the Continent for the
first time, Locke indulged in a good deal of merriment at
the Catholic ceremonies, he pays, in one of his letters to
Strachey, a cheerful tribute to the personal worth of the
Catholic priests.   He had not met, he says, with any
people so good-natured or so civil, and he had received
many courtesies from them, which he should always grate-
fully acknowledge.

Locke returned to England towards the end of February,
1665-6, and was at once offered the post of secretary to
the Earl of Sandwich, who was on the point of setting out
as ambassador to Spain.   He wavered for a short time, but,
though doubtful whether he had not " let slip the minute
that they say every one has once in his life to make himself,"
he finally declined the offer.   Before settling down again
in Oxford, he spent a few weeks in Somersetshire, paying
probably, amongst other visits, one he had promised himself to Strachey at Sutton Court, " a greater rarity than
my travels have afforded me ; for one may go a long way
before one meets a friend."   During his stay in Somersetshire, he attempted to try some experiments in the Men-
dip lead-mines with a barometer which had been sent to
him for the purpose by Boyle.   But the miners and their

wives made a successful resistance. "The sight of the engine and my desire of going down some of their gruffs gave them terrible apprehensions. The women, too, were alarmed, and think us still either projectors or conjurors."

At the beginning of May, Locke was again in his rooms in Oxford. He seems to have lost no time in setting to work afresh on the studies which might qualify him to exercise the profession of medicine. In his letters to Boyle, he makes frequent reference to chemical experiments and to collecting plants for medical purposes.

It is an unexplained circumstance that, notwithstanding a letter to the Hebdomadal Board from Lord Clarendon, then Chancellor of the University, signifying his assent to a dispensation, enabling Locke to accumulate the degrees of Bachelor and Doctor in Medicine, he never took those degrees. The obstacle may have arisen from himself, or, more probably, it may have been due to some sinister influence on the Hebdomadal Board preventing the assent of that body to the required decree. Any way, it is curious that eleven days after the date of Lord Clarendon's letter is dated the dispensation from the Crown (already referred to on page 13), enabling him to retain his studentship, notwithstanding his neglect to enter holy orders.

During the summer of 1666, we are introduced to one of the turning-points in Locke's life—his first acquaintance with Lord Shaftesbury, or, as he then was, Lord Ashley Of the chequered career or the enigmatical character of this celebrated nobleman it is no part of my task to speak. It is enough to say that, as an advocate of religious toleration and an opponent alike of sacerdotal claims in the Church and absolutist principles in the State, he appealed to Locke's warmest and deepest sympathies. The acquaintance was made through David Thomas, an Oxford physician, and the occasion of it was Lord Ashley's coming to Oxford to drink the Astrop waters. The duty of providing these waters (Astrop being a village at some distance from Oxford) seems to have been entrusted by Thomas to Locke, but, there having been some miscarriage, Locke waited on Lord Ashley to excuse the delay. " My lord," says Lady Masham, " in his wonted manner, received him very civilly, accepting his excuse with great easiness, and, when Mr. Locke would have taken his leave of him, would needs have him to stay supper with him, being much pleased with his conversation. But if my lord was pleased with the company of Mr. Locke, Mr. Locke was yet more so with that of my Lord Ashley." The result of this short and apparently accidental interview was the beginning of an intimate friendship, which seems never afterwards to have been broken, and which exercised a decisive influence on the rest of Locke's career.

On September 2 of this year broke out the Great Fire of London, which raged without intermission for three days and nights. Under the date of September 3 we find in Locke's " Register," which was afterwards published in Boyle's *General History of the Air*, this curious entry :— " Dim reddish sunshine. This unusual colour of the air, which, without a cloud appearing, made the sunbeams of a strange red dim light, was very remarkable. We had then heard nothing of the fire of London ; but it appeared afterwards to be the smoke of London, then burning, which, driven this way by an easterly wind, caused this odd phenomenon." The Register, in which this entry is made, begins on June 24, 1666, and contains, with many inter-

missions, the observations made by Locke, in Oxford and
London, up to June 30, 1683, on the readings of the
"thermoscope," the "baroscope," and the "hygroscope,"
together with the direction of the wind and the state of
the weather. It not only affords valuable evidence of
Locke's whereabouts at different times, but also shows the
interest which he took in physical research.

In the early summer of 1667, Locke appears to have
taken up his residence with Lord Ashley in London, and
"from that time," according to Lady Masham, "he was
with my Lord Ashley as a man at home, and lived in that
family much esteemed, not only by my lord, but by all
the friends of the family." His residence in Lord Ashley's
family was, however, probably broken by occasional visits
to Oxford.

To this period of Locke's life may be assigned the
unpublished *Essay concerning Toleration*, which, with
so much other valuable matter, is now for the first time
accessible to the general reader in Mr. Fox-Bourne's *Life*.
This *Essay*, it is not improbable, was written at the suggestion, or for the guidance of Lord Ashley, and so may
have been widely circulated amongst the advocates of
"toleration" and "comprehension"—words which were at
that time in the mouth of every man who took any
interest in religion or politics. As I shall have to speak
expressly of the published *Letters on Toleration*, which
were written about twenty years later, and which contain
substantially the same views as this earlier *Essay*, I shall
not here detain the reader further than by giving him the
general conclusions at which Locke had now arrived.
These may be stated summarily under three heads : first,
"all speculative opinions and religious worship have a
clear title to universal toleration," and in these every man

may use "a perfect uncontrollable liberty, without any guilt or sin at all, provided always that it be all done sincerely and out of conscience to God, according to the best of his knowledge and persuasion;" secondly, "there are some opinions and actions which are in their natural tendency absolutely destructive to human society—as, that faith may be broken with heretics; that one is bound to broach and propagate any opinion he believes himself; and such like; and, in actions, all manner of frauds and injustice—and these the magistrate ought not to tolerate at all;" thirdly, another class of opinions and actions, inasmuch as their "influence to good or bad" depends on "the temper of the state and posture of affairs," "have a right to toleration so far only as they do not interfere with the advantages of the public, or serve any way to disturb the government." The practical result of the discussion is, that while "papists" should not "enjoy the benefit of toleration, because where they have power they think themselves bound to deny it to others," the "fanatics," as the various classes of Protestant Dissenters were then called, should be at least "tolerated," if not "comprehended" in the national church. Indeed, as to "comprehension," Locke lays down the general principle that "your articles in speculative opinions should be few and large, and your ceremonies in worship few and easy—which is latitudinism."

This must have been one of the quietest and happiest periods of Locke's life. He seems to have been unobtrusively pursuing his studies, and gradually making the acquaintance of the great world and of public affairs through the facilities which his residence with Lord Ashley afforded him. Both his own occupations and his relations to the Ashley family appear to have been of a very miscellaneous kind.   Medicine, philosophy, and politics engaged his attention by turns.   To Lord Ashley and his family he was at once general adviser, doctor, and friend.   In June, 1668, after consulting various other medical men, he performed on Lord Ashley a difficult operation for the purpose of removing an "imposthume in the breast," and is said thus to have saved his life.   To the only child, Anthony Ashley, he acted as tutor.   But, by the time the youth was seventeen, Locke was entrusted with a far more delicate business than his tuition.   This was no less than finding him a wife.   After other young ladies had been considered and rejected, Locke accompanied his charge on a visit to the Earl of Rutland, at Belvoir Castle, and negotiated a match with the Earl's daughter, the Lady Dorothy Manners.   The match seems to have been a happy one ; and Locke continued his services of general utility to the Ashley family by acting on more than one occasion as Lady Dorothy's medical attendant.   On the 26th of February, 1670-1, he assisted at the birth of a son and heir, Anthony, who subsequently became third Earl of Shaftesbury, and who, as the author of the *Characteristics*, occupies a position of no inconsiderable importance in the history of English philosophy. It is on the evidence of this Earl of Shaftesbury that we learn the share taken by Locke in effecting the union of his father and mother.   "My father was too young and inexperienced to choose a wife for himself, and my grandfather too much in business to choose one for him."   The consequence was, that "all was thrown upon Mr. Locke, who being already so good a judge of men, my grandfather doubted not of his equal judgment in women.   He departed from him, entrusted and sworn, as Abraham's head servant 'that ruled over all that he had,' and went into a far country 'to seek for his son a wife,' whom he as successfully found."

Though so much of Locke's time seems to have been spent on medical studies and practice, he possessed no regular qualification. In 1670 another attempt had been made, but in vain, to procure him the Doctor of Medicine's degree from the University of Oxford. Lord Ashley successfully enlisted the good services of the Duke of Ormond, the Chancellor of the University ; but on learning the opposition of Dean Fell and Dr. Allestree, Locke desired his patron to withdraw the application. Both now and on the former occasion, alluded to above (p. 16), the opposition was probably based on Locke's tendencies, known or suspected, to liberal views in religion ; nor would the connexion with Lord Ashley be at all likely to mitigate the sternness of the college and university authorities. It had, of course, all along been open to him to proceed to the Doctor's degree in the ordinary way, by attending lectures and performing exercises; and whether he was prevented from doing so by the tediousness of the process, by the hope of attaining the degree through a shorter and easier method, or by a certain amount of indecision as to whether after all he would adopt the medical profession, we cannot say. Afterwards, we shall see, he proceeded to the degree of Bachelor of Medicine, but whether in the ordinary course, or by dispensation, is not known.

As connected with Locke's medical pursuits, I may here mention his friendship with Sydenham. We do not know when the acquaintance commenced, but Sydenham writing to Boyle, so early as April 2, 1668, speaks of "my friend Mr. Locke." That Sydenham entertained great respect for the medical skill and judgment of Locke—who appears to have accompanied him in his visits to his

patients, and, in turn, to have availed himself of Sydenham's assistance in attending the Ashley household—there
can be no doubt. Writing to Mapletoft, their common
friend, and a physician of some eminence, in 1676, he
says : "You know how thoroughly my method [of curing
fevers] is approved of by an intimate and common friend
of ours, and one who has closely and exhaustively examined the subject—I mean Mr. John Locke, a man whom,
in the acuteness of his intellect, in the steadiness of his
judgment, and in the simplicity, that is, in the excellence,
of his manners, I confidently declare to have amongst the
men of our own time few equals and no superior." A
number of notes and papers, still extant, attest the interest
which Locke now took in medical studies, and the hopes
with which he looked forward to improvements in medical
practice. That the sympathy between him and Sydenham
was very close, is evident from the writings of both.

But, meanwhile, he was also busy with other pursuits.
One of these was the administration, under Ashley, and
the other "lords proprietors," of the colony of Carolina.
In 1663 this colony had been granted by Charles the
Second to eight "lords proprietors," of whom Ashley was
one. Locke, when he went to live in Ashley's family,
appears to have become, though without any formal appointment, a sort of chief secretary and manager to the
association. A vast amount of miscellaneous business
seems to have been transacted by him in this capacity ;
but what to us would be most interesting, if we could
determine it, would be the share he took in drawing up
the document entitled, "The Fundamental Constitutions
of Carolina," issued on the 1st of March, 1669-70. Many
of the articles, embodying, as they do, a sort of modified
feudalism, must have been distasteful to Locke, and it is

hardly possible to suppose that he was the originator of
them. But perhaps we may trace his hand in the articles on
religion, between which and his views, as stated in his unpublished papers written before and his published works
written after this time, there is a large amount of correspondence. No man was to be permitted to be a freeman
of Carolina unless he acknowledged a God, and agreed that
God was to be publicly and solemnly worshipped. But
within these limits any seven persons might constitute a
church, provided that they upheld the duty of every man, if
called on, to bear witness to the truth, and agreed on some
external symbol by which such witness might be signified.
Any one, however, who did not belong to some such communion was to be regarded as outside the protection of
the law. The members of one church were not to molest
or persecute those of another; and no man was to "use
any reproachful, reviling, or abusive language against the
religion of any church or profession, that being the certain
way of disturbing the peace, and of hindering the conver-
sion of any to the truth." Amongst the miscellaneous
provisions in this code is one strictly forbidding any one
to plead before a court of justice for money or reward; and
another, enacting that " every freeman of Carolina shall
have absolute power and authority over his negro slaves,
of what opinion or religion soever."

In 1668 Locke was elected a Fellow of the Royal
Society, and in 1669 and 1672 was placed on the Council,
but he never appears to have taken much part in the proceedings of the society. On the other hand, there seem
to have been certain less formal meetings of a few friends,
constituting possibly a sort of club, in the discussions of
which he took a more active share. It was at one of these
meetings that the conversation took place which led to

Locke's writing his famous *Essay* (see page 127). According to a marginal note made by Sir James Tyrrell in his copy of the first edition, now in the British Museum, the discussion on this occasion turned on "the principles of morality and revealed religion." The date of this memorable meeting was, according to the same authority, the winter of 1673 ; but according to Lady Masham, it was 1670 or 1671. Anyway, there is an entry on the main subject of the *Essay* in Locke's Common-place Book, beginning " Sic cogitavit de intellectu humano Johannes Locke, anno 1671." In this brief entry the origin of all knowledge is referred to sense, and " sensible qualities" are stated to be " the simplest ideas we have and the first object of our understanding "—a theory which, as we shall hereafter see, was supplemented in the *Essay* by the addition to the ultimate sources of knowledge of simple ideas of reflection. The *Essay* itself was not published till nearly twenty years after this date, in 1690.

Locke's health had never been strong, and, in the years 1670-2 he seems to have suffered much from a troublesome cough, indicative of disease of the lungs. Connected with this illness was a short journey which he made in France, in the suite of the Countess of Northumberland, in the autumn of 1672. Soon after his return, his patron, who had lately been created Earl of Shaftesbury, was appointed to the highest office of the State, the Lord High Chancellorship of England. Locke shared in his good fortune, and was made Secretary of Presentations—that is, of the Chancellor's church patronage—with a salary of 300*l.* a year. The modern reader, especially when he recollects Locke's intimacy with Shaftesbury, is surprised to find that he dined at the Steward's table, that he was expected to attend prayers three times a day, and that, when the Chancellor drove out in state, he was accustomed, with the other secretaries, to walk by the side of the coach, while, as "my lord" got in and out, he "went before him bareheaded." The distinctions of rank were, however, far more marked in those days than at present, and the high officers of state were still surrounded with much of the elaborate ceremonial which had obtained in the times of the Tudors.

To the period of Locke's excursion in France, or that immediately succeeding it, we may refer a free translation —or rather, adaptation—of three of the *Essais de Morale* of Pierre Nicole, a well-known Jansenist, and the friend of Pascal and Arnauld. These *Essays*, which were translated for the use of the Countess of Shaftesbury, were apparently not designed for publication, and, in fact, were first given to the world by Dr. Hancock, in 1828. They are mainly remarkable as affording evidence of the depth and sincerity of Locke's religious convictions.

Routine and official duties now occupied much of his time, and must have interfered sadly with his favourite studies. From discussing the tangled and ambiguous politics of this period I purposely refrain ; but there is one official act, recorded of Locke at this time, which places him in so incongruous a light that his biographer can hardly pass it over in silence. At the opening of the Parliament which met on February 4, 1672-3, Shaftesbury, amplifying the King's Speech, made, though it is said unwillingly and with much concern, his famous defence of the Dutch war, and his attack on the Dutch nation, culminating in the words " Delenda est Carthago." Locke, we are sorry to find, though the act was a purely ministerial one, stood at his elbow with a written copy, to prompt him in case of failure.

On the 9th of November, 1673, Shaftesbury, who had incurred the displeasure of the King by his support of the Test Bill, and who was now looked on as one of the principal leaders of the Anti-Catholic party, was summarily dismissed from the Chancellorship. Locke, of course, lost at the same time the Secretaryship of Presentations ; but he did not, as meaner men might have done, try to in- sinuate himself into wealth and power through other avenues. "When my grandfather," says the third Earl of Shaftesbury, "quitted the Court and began to be in danger from it, Mr. Locke now shared with him in dan- gers, as before in honours and advantages. He entrusted him with his secretest negotiations, and made use of his assistant pen in matters that nearly concerned the State and were fit to be made public."

Locke's connexion with the affairs of the colony of Carolina has already been mentioned. Business of this kind, owing to his relations with Shaftesbury, multiplied upon him, and on the 15th of October, 1673, shortly be- fore Shaftesbury's fall, he was sworn in as Secretary to the Council of Trade and Foreign Plantations, with a salary of 500*l.* a year. This office he retained, notwith- standing the fall of his patron, till the dissolution of the Council on the 12th of March, 1674-5 ; but it appears that his salary was never paid.

On February 6, 1674-5, Locke proceeded to the degree of Bachelor of Medicine, having already been appointed to, or more probably promised, a Faculty Studentship at Ch. Ch., or, as Dean Prideaux, who had no love for him, puts it, "having wriggled into Ireland's faculty place." It is curious that his name does not appear in the Ch. Ch. books among the Faculty Students till the second quarter of 1675, and during that and the two subsequent quarters it is erased. The first time the name occurs without an erasure is in the first quarter of 1676. That there was much irregularity in the mode of appointing to College places at this time is evident.

His studentship being now secure, Lord Shaftesbury having, for a consideration in ready money, granted him an annuity of 100*l.* a year, and his estates in Somersetshire, as well as one or two loans and mortgages, bringing him in a modest sum in addition, Locke, notwithstanding the non-payment of his salary as Secretary to the Council of Trade and Plantations, must have been in fairly comfortable circumstances. He was dispensed from the necessity of practising a profession, and, being also relieved from the pressure of public affairs, was free to follow his bent. It is probably to the leisure almost enforced upon him by the weakness of his health as well as by the turn which public affairs had taken, and rendered possible by the independence of his position, that we are indebted for the maturity of reflection which forms so characteristic a feature of his subsequent writings.

CHAPTER III.

THE state of Locke's health had long rendered it desirable
that he should reside in a warmer climate, and his release
from official duties now removed any obstacle that there
might formerly have been to his absence from England.
The place which he selected for his retirement was Montpellier, at that time the most usual place of resort for
invalids who were able to leave their own country. He
left London about the middle of November, 1675, with
one if not more companions, and, after experiencing the
ordinary inconveniences of travel in those days of slow
locomotion and poor inns, arrived at Paris on Nov. 24,
and at Lyons on Dec. 11. At Lyons, he remarks of the
library at the Jesuits' College that it " is the best that
ever I saw, except Oxford, being one very high oblong
square, with a gallery round, to come at the books." As
before, in the North of Germany, so now in the South of
France, he is a diligent observer of everything of interest,
whether in the way of customs, occupations, or buildings,
that falls in his way. He reached Montpellier on Christmas Day, and, except when making short excursions in
the neighbourhood, resided there continuously till the
early spring of 1677, a period of fourteen months. At

Montpellier I have not been able to find any trace of him,
either in the library or elsewhere, but his journal shows
that he was much interested in the trade and products of
the country, as well as in the objects which usually excite
the curiosity of travellers.   At Shaftesbury's instigation
he wrote a little treatise, entitled, " Observations upon
the Growth and Culture of Vines and Olives, the Production of Silk, and the Preservation of Fruits."   It is
curious that this small tract was never published till
1766.   It enumerates no less than forty-one varieties of
grapes, and thirteen varieties of olives, which were grown
in the neighbourhood of Montpellier.   The ceremonial
and doings of the States of Languedoc attracted Locke's
attention, but he does not seem to have been present at
their deliberations.   He witnessed, however, their devotions at the Church of Notre Dame, and remarks that the
Cardinal Archbishop of Narbonne, who took part in the
offices, kept " talking every now and then, and laughing
with the bishops next him."   The increasing incidence of
the taxation on the lower and middle orders, and the
growing poverty of the people, were topics which could
hardly fail to arrest the attention of any intelligent traveller at that time.   " The rent of lands in France is
fallen one half in these few years, by reason of the poverty
of the people.   Merchants and handicraftsmen pay near
half their gains."   Among the more interesting entries in
his journal are the following :—March 18th (N.S.).
"Monsieur Rennaie, a gentleman of the town, in whose
house Sir J. Rushworth lay, about four years ago, sacrificed a child to the devil—a child of a servant of his own,
upon a design to get the devil to be his friend and help
him to get some money.   Several murders committed
here since I came, and more attempted ; one by a brother

on his sister, in the house where I lay." March 22nd
(N.S.) : "The new philosophy of Des Cartes prohibited
to be taught in universities, schools, and academies." It
is plain from the journal that Locke's mind was now
busy with the class of questions which were afterwards
treated in the Essay ; reflections on space, the extent of
possible knowledge, the objects and modes of study, &c.,
being curiously interspersed with his notes of travel. In
respect of health, he does not seem to have benefited
much by his stay at Montpellier, which, as before stated,
he left in the early spring of 1677. By slow stages he
travelled to Paris, where he joined a pupil, the son of Sir
John Banks, who had been commended to his supervision
by Shaftesbury. This tutorial engagement lasted for
nearly two years, and, in consequence of it, Locke remained
in France longer than he had originally intended. In a
letter written to his old friend Mapletoft from Paris in
June, 1677, after some playful allusions to Mapletoft's love
affairs, he says :—" My health is the only mistress I have
a long time courted, and is so coy a one that I think it will
take up the remainder of my days to obtain her good
graces and keep her in good humour." There can be no
question that, at this time, the state of his health was a
matter of very serious concern to him, and it may possibly
have been the cause of his not marrying. While in Paris
he probably took a pretty complete holiday, seeing the
sights, however, making occasional excursions, forming
new acquaintances, and exercising a general supervision
over the education of his young charge.

At the end of June, 1678, Locke, accompanied probably
by his pupil, left Paris with the view of making his way
leisurely to Montpellier, and thence to Rome. He travelled westward by way of Orleans, Blois, and Angers.

On the banks of the Loire he noticed the poverty-stricken appearance of the country. " Many of the towns they call bourgs ; but, considering how poor and few the houses in most of them are, would in England scarce amount to villages. The houses generally were but one story. . . . The gentlemen's seats, of which we saw many, were most of them rather bearing marks of decay than of thriving and being well kept." Montpellier was reached early in October, and, after a short stay there, he went on to Lyons, with the view of commencing his journey to Rome. But the depth of the snow on Mont Cenis was fatal to this design. Twice Locke had formed plans to visit Rome, " the time set, the company agreed," and both times he had been disappointed. " Were I not accustomed," he says, " to have fortune to dispose of me contrary to my design and expectation, I should be very angry to be thus turned out of my way, when I made sure in a few days to mount the Capitol and trace the footsteps of the Scipios and the Cæsars." He had now nothing left but to turn back to Paris, where he remained till the following April. Here he seems to have spent his time in the same miscellaneous occupations as before. In the journal we find the following entry, dated Feb. 13 :— " I saw the library of M. de Thou, a great collection of choice, well-bound books, which are now to be sold ; amongst others, a Greek manuscript, written by one Angelot, by which Stephens' Greek characters were first made." De Thou, the celebrated historian of his own times, is better known under his Latinized name, Thuanus. On a Friday, he notes :—" The observation of Lent at Paris is come almost to nothing. Meat is openly to be had in the shambles, and a dispensation commonly to be had from the curate without difficulty. People of sense

laugh at it, and in Italy itself, for twenty sous, a dispensation is certainly to be had." Then follows an amusing
story of "that Bishop of Bellay, who has writ so much
against monks and monkery."

"A devout lady being sick, and besieged by the Carmes, made
her will and gave them all : the Bishop of Bellay coming to see
her, after it was done, asked whether she had made her will ;
she answered yes, and told him how ; he convinced her it was
not well, and she, desiring to alter it, found a difficulty how
to do it, being so beset by the friars. The bishop bid her not
trouble herself for it, but presently took order that two notaries,
habited as physicians, should come to her, who being by her
bedside, the bishop told the company it was convenient all should
withdraw ; and so the former will was revoked, and a new one
made and put into the bishop's hands. The lady dies, the
Carmes produce their will, and for some time the bishop lets
them enjoy the pleasure of their inheritance ; but at last, taking
out the other will, he says to them, 'Mes frères, you are the
sons of Elijah, children of the Old Testament, and have no share
in the New.' "

It may have been the influence of fashion and the
eager thirst for reputation, which were so rife in Parisian
society, that inspired, shortly after Locke's return to
Paris, the following reflections, as profound as they are
true :—

"The principal spring from which the actions of men take
their rise, the rule they conduct them by, and the end to which
they direct them, seems to be credit and reputation, and that
which, at any rate, they avoid is in the greatest part shame and
disgrace. This makes the Hurons and other people of Canada
with such constancy endure inexpressible torments ; this makes
merchants in one country and soldiers in another ; this puts men
upon school divinity in one country and physics and mathematics in another ; this cuts out the dresses for the women, and

makes the fashions for the men, and makes them endure the
inconveniences of all. . . . . Religions are upheld by this and
factions maintained, and the shame of being disesteemed by
those with whom one hath lived, and to whom one would recom-
mend oneself, is the great source and director of most of the
actions of men. . . . He therefore that would govern the world
well, had need consider rather what fashions he makes than
what laws; and to bring anything into use he need only give
it reputation."

Leaving Paris on the 22nd of April, 1679, Locke
arrived, after his long absence, in London on the 30th of
the same month.   In the political world, much had happened whilst he had been away.   Shaftesbury, already
in disgrace when he left England, had been imprisoned
in the Tower for a year ; but, by a sudden turn of fortune,
was now reinstated in office as President of the newly-
created Council. Of the circumstances which had brought
about this change, the story of the Popish Plot, the discovery of the King's nefarious negotiations with Louis
XIV., and the impeachment of Danby, it is not necessary
here to speak.   That Shaftesbury, when he saw the pro
spect of restoration to power, should wish to avail himself,
as before, of Locke's advice and services, was only to be
expected, and it was the expression of this desire which
had hastened Locke's return to England.   What, however, were the exact relations between the new Lord
President and his former secretary during Shaftesbury's
second tenure of office we are not informed.   That the
intercourse between them was close and frequent, there
can be no doubt, and, during the summer months of
1679, Locke again resided in his patron's house.   But
the king soon felt himself strong enough to reassert
his own will.   Under date of the 15th of October, we

read in the Privy Council Book, " The Earl of Shaftesbury's name was struck out of this list by his Majesty's
command in Council."   Consequently, Shaftesbury was
again in opposition, and Locke, though still his adviser
and friend, and frequently an inmate of one or other of
his houses, was released from the pressure of official business.   One of his principal cares at this time was the
supervision of the education of Shaftesbury's grandson.
The father, Locke's former pupil, " born a shapeless lump,
like anarchy," seems to have been but a poor creature, and
the little Anthony, when only three years old, was made
over to the formal guardianship of his grandfather. Locke,
though not his instructor, seems to have kept a vigilant
eye on the boy's studies and discipline, as well as on his
health and bodily training.   If we may trust the memory
of the third earl, writing when in middle life, Locke's
care was extended to his brothers and sisters as well as
to himself.   " In our education," he says, " Mr. Locke
governed according to his own principles, since published
by him " [in the *Thoughts on Education*], " and with
such success that we all of us came to full years with strong
and healthy constitutions—my own the worst, though
never faulty till of late.   I was his more peculiar charge,
being, as eldest son, taken by my grandfather and bred
under his immediate care, Mr. Locke having the absolute
direction of my education, and to whom, next my immediate parents, as I must own the greatest obligation, so I
have ever preserved the highest gratitude and duty."   The
admiration and gratitude which the author of the *Characteristics* felt for his tutor did not, however, prevent him
from criticizing freely Locke's *Theory of Ethics*, and pro-
nouncing it " a very poor philosophy."   Of the *Essay*, as
a whole, notwithstanding his vigorous protest on this par-

ticular point, Shaftesbury seems to have had as high an
opinion as of its author. "It may as well qualify for
business and the world as for the sciences and a university. No one has done more towards the recalling of
philosophy from barbarity into use and practice of the
world, and into the company of the better and politer
sort, who might well be ashamed of it in its other dress.
No one has opened a better or clearer way to reasoning."
(See the Letters of the third Earl of Shaftesbury to a
Student at the University, Letters I., VIII.)

Of the parliament which met at Oxford on the 21st of
March, 1680-1, Locke was a close, and must have been
an anxious, observer. He himself occupied his rooms at
Christ Church, and for Shaftesbury's use he obtained the
house of the celebrated mathematician, Dr. Wallis. The
fullest account we have of the earlier proceedings of this
parliament are contained in a letter from Locke to
Stringer, Shaftesbury's Secretary. It was prematurely
dissolved on the 28th of March, Charles having succeeded in obtaining supplies from the French king instead
of from his own subjects, and no other parliament was
summoned during the remainder of the reign.

So suspicious of treachery had the rival parties in the
State now become, that most of the members of the
Oxford parliament had been attended by armed servants,
while the king was protected by a body of guards. The
political tension was, of course, by no means relaxed,
when it became plain that the king intended to govern
without a parliament, and we can hardly feel surprised
that ministers took the initiative in trying to silence their
opponents. On the 2nd of July, 1681, Shaftesbury was
arrested in his London house on a charge of high treason,
and, after a brief examination before the Council, was

committed to the tower. Notwithstanding many attempts, he failed to obtain a trial till Nov. 24, when he was indicted before a special commission at the Old Bailey. The grand jury, amidst the plaudits of the spectators, threw out the bill, and on the 1st of December following he was released on bail. Shaftesbury's acquittal was received in London, and throughout the country, with acclamations of joy, but his triumph was only a brief one. The rest of his story is soon told. In the summer of 1682, Shaftesbury, Monmouth, Russell, and a few others, began to concert measures for a general rising against the king. The scheme was, of course, discovered, and Shaftesbury, knowing that, from the new composition of the juries, he would have no chance of escape if another indictment were preferred against him, took to flight, and concealed himself for some weeks in obscure houses in the city and in Wapping. Meanwhile he tried, from his hiding-places, to foment an insurrection, but, when he found that the day which had been fixed on for the general rising had been postponed, he determined to seek safety for himself by escaping to Holland. After some adventures on the way, he reached Amsterdam in the beginning of December. To preserve him from extradition, he was on his petition admitted a citizen of Amsterdam, and might thus, like Locke, have lived to see the Revolution, but on the 21st of January, 1682-3, he died, in excruciating agonies, of gout in the stomach.

There is no evidence to implicate Locke in Shaftesbury's design of setting the Duke of Monmouth on the throne, though it is difficult to suppose that he was not acquainted with it. Any way, in the spring of 1681-2, he seems to have been engaged in some mysterious political movements, the nature of which is unknown to us. Humphrey

Prideaux, afterwards Dean of Norwich, in his gossiping letters to John Ellis, afterwards an Under-Secretary of State, frequently mentions Locke, who was at this time residing in Oxford.   These notices were probably in answer to queries from Ellis, who was already in the employment of the government.   From Prideaux's letters (recently published by the Camden Society) I extract a few passages, interesting not only as throwing light on Locke's mode of life at this period in Oxford, but also as showing the estimate of him formed by a political enemy who was a member of the same college :—

"*March* 14, 1681 (o.s.).—John Locke lives a very cunning and unintelligible life here, being two days in town and three out; and no one knows where he goes, or when he goes, or when he returns.   Certainly there is some Whig intrigue a managing ; but here not a word of politics comes from him, nothing of news or anything else concerning our present affairs, as if he were not at all concerned in them.

"*March* 19, 1681 (o.s.).—Where J. L. goes I cannot by any means learn, all his voyages being so cunningly contrived.   He hath in his last sally been absent at least ten days, where I cannot learn.   Last night he returned ; and sometimes he himself goes out and leaves his man behind, who shall then to be often seen in the quadrangle to make people believe his master is at home, for he will let no one come to his chamber, and therefore it is not certain when he is there or when he is absent. I fancy there are projects afoot.

"*October* 24, 1682.—John Locke lives very quietly with us, and not a word ever drops from his mouth that discovers anything of his heart within.   Now his master is fled, I suppose we shall have him altogether.   He seems to be a man of very good converse, and that we have of him with content ; as for what else he is he keeps it to himself, and therefore troubles not us with it nor we him."

After Shaftesbury's dismissal from the Presidentship of

the Council, Locke must have had a considerable amount
of leisure.   The state of his health, however, and the con-
sequent necessity of his frequently changing his residence,
must have interfered a good deal with the progress of his
studies.   It is plain from his correspondence that he still
took a lively interest in scientific and medical pursuits,
nor does he appear to have yet given up the hope of
practising medicine in a regular way.   By his friends he
was usually called Dr. Locke, and at the period of life
we are now considering he still continued to attend cases,
and to make elaborate notes of treatment and diagnosis.

It is probable that about this time Locke wrote the
first of the *Two Treatises on Government,* which were
published in 1690.   Materials for the Essay were, undoubtedly, being slowly accumulated, and on a variety of
questions, political, educational, ethical, theological, and
philosophical, his views were being gradually matured.
Several pamphlets of a political character were, during
these years, attributed to him, but we have his own
solemn asseveration, in a letter written to the Earl of
Pembroke in November, 1684, that he was not the
author " of any pamphlet or treatise whatever, in part
good, bad, or indifferent ;" that is, of course, of any published pamphlet or treatise, for he had already written a
good deal in the way of essays, reflections, and common-
places.

After Shaftesbury's flight, Locke must have found his
position becoming more and more unpleasant.   During
the year 1682 he had resided pretty constantly in Oxford,
but we can well understand that Oxford was not then a very
eligible place of residence for a whig and a latitudinarian.
He appears to have left it for good at the end of June or
beginning of July, 1683, and to have retired for a while

into Somersetshire. Shortly afterwards, however, he
quitted England altogether, and when we next hear of
him it is in Holland. That he was implicated in the Rye
House plot is, on every ground, most improbable, notwithstanding the malicious insinuations of Prideaux to the
contrary. Nor is there any evidence that he had any
concern with the more respectable conspiracy of Monmouth, Russell, and Sidney. But in those times of
plots and counter-plots, and arbitrary interference with
the courts of justice, any man who was in opposition to
the government might well be in fear for his life or
liberty. Specially would this be the case with Locke,
who was well known as a friend and adherent of Shaftesbury. Moreover, had he been thrown into prison, the
state of his health was such that his life would probably
have been endangered. His flight, therefore, affords no
countenance whatsoever to the supposition that he had
been engaged in treasonable designs against the government. It would, I conceive, be no stain on Locke's
character, had he, in those days of misgovernment and
oppression, conspired to effect by violent means a change
in the succession, or even a transference of the crown.
But the fact that there is no evidence of his having done
so removes almost all excuse for the tyrannical act which
I am presently about to describe. In connexion with
Locke's flight to Holland, it may be mentioned that the
idea of leaving England was by no means new to him.
The proposal to emigrate together to Carolina or the
Île de Bourbon, possibly, however, thrown out half in
jest, is a frequent topic in the correspondence with his
French friend, Thoynard, during the two or three years
succeeding his return from France. That he was becoming
disgusted with the political game then being played in

England, and despondent as to the future of his country, is evident from several letters written by him at this time.

The account of Locke's life in Holland may be deferred to the next chapter. It will be convenient here to tell the story of his expulsion from Christ Church, which marks the issue of his connexion with Shaftesbury, and of the part which he had so far taken in English politics. We have already seen that he was suspected of having written a number of political pamphlets against the government. This suspicion was not unnatural, Locke being a literary man and a well-known friend of Shaftesbury. After his retirement to Holland, the suspicion of his having written various pamphlets, supposed to have been printed in that country and surreptitiously conveyed into England, was one which very naturally occurred, and, according to Prideaux, he was now specially suspected of having written "a most bitter libel, published in Holland in English, Dutch, and French, called a Hue and Cry after the Earl of Essex's murder." But the government had no proof of these surmises, and therefore no right to take action upon them. Their suspicions were, however, probably sharpened by the malicious reports of their spies in Oxford, and by the not unlikely supposition that Locke was taking part in the intrigues, on behalf of Monmouth, now being carried on in Holland. For the latter suspicion, as for the one with regard to the authorship of the pamphlets, it happens that there was no justification, but it is impossible to deny that there was some *primâ facie* ground for it. Compared with other arbitrary acts of the reigns of Charles II. and James II., the measures taken against Locke do not seem exceptionally severe, utterly abhorrent as they would doubtless be to the usages of a constitutional age.

About fourteen or fifteen months had elapsed since his disappearance from England, when, on the 6th of November, 1684, Lord Sunderland signified to Dr. Fell, Dean of Christ Church, who was also Bishop of Oxford, the pleasure of the king that Locke should be removed from his studentship, asking the Dean at the same time to specify "the method of doing it." "The method" adopted by the Dean was to attach a " moneo " to the screen in the college hall, summoning Locke to appear on the 1st of January following, to answer the charges against him. After admitting that Locke, as having a physician's place among the students, was not obliged to residence, and that he was abroad upon want of health, the Dean, in his reply to Sunderland, proceeds to show his readiness to accommodate himself to the requirements of the court : "Notwithstanding that, I have summoned him to return home, which is donè with this prospect, that if he comes not back, he will be liable to expulsion for contumacy ; if he does, he will be answerable to your lordship for what he shall be found to have done amiss." Ingenious, however, as the "method" was, it was not expeditious enough to satisfy the court. A second letter from Sunderland, enjoining Locke's immediate expulsion, was at once despatched. This curious document is still shown in the Christ Church library, and, as I have never seen an exact transcript of it, I here subjoin one :—

    " To the Right Reverend Father in God, John, Lord Bishop
        of Oxon, Dean of Christ-Church, and our trusty and well-
        beloved the Chapter there.
    " Right Reverend Father in God, and trusty and well-beloved,
we greet you well. Whereas we have received information of
the factious and disloyall behaviour of   Lock, one of the
students of that our Colledge; we have thought fit hereby to

signify our will and pleasure to you, that you forthwith remove
him from his said student's place, and deprive him of all the
rights and advantages thereunto belonging.   For which this
shall be your warrant.   And so we bid you heartily farewell.

"Given at our Court at Whitehall, 11th day of November,
1684, in the six and thirtieth year of our Reigne.

"By his Majesty's command,

"SUNDERLAND."

On the 16th of November the Dean signified that his
Majesty's command was fully executed, whereupon Lord
Sunderland acquainted him that his Majesty was well
satisfied with the college's ready obedience.

Thus the most celebrated man, perhaps, that Oxford
has sheltered within her walls since the Reformation was
summarily ejected at the dictation of a corrupt and arbitrary court.   The Dean and Chapter might have won our
admiration, had they resisted the royal command, as was
done in the next reign by the Fellows of Magdalen
College, but it was hardly to be expected that they should
risk their own goods and liberties in attempting to afford
a protection which, after all, would have been almost
certainly attempted in vain.   Moreover, as Lord Gren-
ville (*Oxford and Locke*) has pointed out, Christ Church
being a royal foundation, the Dean and Chapter might
well regard the king as having full power either to appoint
or remove any member of the foundation, and themselves
as only registering his decree.   The same power, as we
have already seen, had been exercised in Locke's favour
by the dispensation from entering holy orders accorded by
the crown in 1666.

After the Revolution, Locke petitioned William the
Third for the restitution of his studentship, but "finding," according to Lady Masham, that "it would give

great disturbance to the society, and dispossess the person that was in his place, he desisted from that pretension."

In Fell's first letter to Sunderland, he speaks of Locke's extreme reserve and taciturnity. As this seems to have been one of his distinguishing characteristics, and as the passage is otherwise remarkable, as showing the vigilance with which Locke was watched at Oxford, I give it at length :—

" I have for divers years had an eye upon him; but so close has his guard been on himself that, after several strict inquiries, I may confidently affirm there is not any one in the College, however familiar with him, who has heard him speak a word either against or so much as concerning the Government; and although very frequently, both in public and in private, discourses have been purposely introduced to the disparagement of his master, the Earl of Shaftesbury, his party and designs, he could never be provoked to take any notice or discover in word or look the least concern; so that I believe there is not in the world such a master of taciturnity and passion."

This account of Locke's reserve, as well as the illustration here incidentally afforded of the abominable system of college espionage which then prevailed in Oxford, is amply confirmed by Prideaux's letters to Ellis. In the *Thoughts on Education* parents and tutors are recommended to mould children betimes to this mastery over their tongues. But the gift of silence was exercised by Locke only in those matters where other men have no right to be inquisitive or curious—matters of private concernment and of individual opinion. In conversation on general topics, he seems always to have been open and copious. His taciturnity, though the effect of prudence and self-control, was certainly not due to any lack of geniality or any want of sympathy with others.

CHAPTER IV.

Locke must have landed in Holland in one of the autumn
months of 1683, being then about fifty-one years of age.
We are not able, however, to trace any of his movements
till the January of 1683-4, when he was present, by in-
vitation of Peter Guenellon, the principal physician of
Amsterdam, at the dissection of a lioness which had been
killed by the intense cold of the winter.

Through Guenellon, whom he had met during his stay
in Paris, he must have made the acquaintance of the
principal literary and scientific men at that time residing
in or near Amsterdam. Amongst these was Philip van
Limborch, then professor of theology among the Arminians
or Remonstrants. The Arminians (called Remonstrants on
account of the remonstrance which they had presented to
the States-General in 1610) were the latitudinarians of
Holland, and, though they had been condemned by the
Synod of Dort in 1619, and had been subjected to a
bitter persecution by the Calvinist clergy for some years
following, were now a fairly numerous body, possessing a
theological seminary, and exercising a considerable influence, not only in their own country, but over the minds

of the more liberal theologians throughout Europe. The undogmatic, tolerant, and, if I may use the expression, ethical character of the Remonstrant theology must have had great attractions for Locke, and he and Limborch, united by many common sentiments, subsequently became fast friends.

In the autumn of 1684 Locke made a tour of the country, noting, as was usual with him, all objects and matters of interest, and evidently benefiting much in health by the diversion of travelling. Indeed, we are somewhat surprised to hear that his health derived more advantage from the air of Holland than from that of Montpellier. What, however, he put down to climate was, perhaps, at least equally due to pleasant companionship, and to the variety of interests—political, commercial, literary, and theological—which the Dutch nation at that time so pre-eminently afforded. Amongst the objects which attracted his attention was a sect of communistic mystics established near Leeuwarden. " They receive," he says, " all ages, sexes, and degrees, upon approbation. They live all in common ; and whoever is admitted is to give with himself all he has to Christ the Lord—that is, the Church—to be managed by officers appointed by the Church. These people, however, were very shy to give an account of themselves to strangers, and they appeared inclined to dispense their instruction only to those whom ' the Lord,' as they say, ' had disposed to it,' and in whom they saw ' signs of grace ; ' which ' signs of grace ' seem to me to be, at last, a perfect submission to the will and rules of their pastor, Mr. Yonn, who, if I mistake not, has established to himself a perfect empire over them. For though their censures and all their administrations be in appearance in their Church, yet it is easy to perceive how at last it determines in him. He is *dominus factotum;* and though I believe they are, generally speaking, people of very good and exemplary lives, yet the tone of voice, manner, and fashion of those I conversed with seemed to make one suspect a little of Tartuffe." After Locke's experiences of the Puritan ministers in his early life, the character of Mr. Yonn was, probably, by no means new to him, though he now repeated his acquaintance with it under novel circumstances.

In November Locke was again in Amsterdam, and here he heard of Dr. Fell's " moneo," summoning him back to Christ Church. At first it would seem that he resolved to comply with it, but the intelligence of the " moneo" must soon have been followed by that of his deprivation, and thus he was saved from the dangers which might have befallen him had he returned to England. In more ways than one, his continued absence abroad was probably an advantage to him. " In Holland," says Lady Masham, " he had full leisure to prosecute his thoughts on the subject of *Human Understanding*—a work which, in probability, he never would have finished had he continued in England." The winter of this year was spent in Utrecht and devoted to study—probably to the preparation of the *Essay on Human Understanding.* But this quiet mode of life was quickly coming to an end. On the 6th of February, 1684-5, Charles the Second had died ; and, though the succession of the Duke of York was at first undisputed, Monmouth, the natural son of the late king, was soon persuaded by his impatient and injudicious followers to head the insurrection which resulted in his defeat and execution. From Monmouth's intrigues Locke had always held aloof, "having no such high opinion of

the Duke of Monmouth as to expect anything from his
undertaking." But prudence, in those days of fierce political hatred and unblushing fabrications, was often of
very little avail. Locke was well known as an adherent
of Shaftesbury, and Shaftesbury had long and ardently
favoured Monmouth's pretensions. Moreover, stories
tending to discredit him with the advisers of the Court,
and to connect his name with the plots of the other exiles,
were probably circulating pretty freely at this time.
On the 7th of May—a few days after Argyle had set out
on his ill-starred expedition to Scotland, and while Monmouth was still preparing for his descent on the west
coast of England—Colonel Skelton, who had been sent
over as a special envoy to the Hague, presented to the
States-General a list of persons regarded as dangerous by
the English Government, and demanded their surrender.
On this list Locke's name stood last, having been added,
we are told, by Sir George Downing, the English representative at the Dutch Court, but whether or not in pur-
suance of further instructions from home we do not know.
Locke was at this time living at Utrecht, and it was at
once arranged that he should be concealed in the house
of Dr. Veen of Amsterdam, the father-in-law of his old
acquaintance, Dr. Guenellon. Though it was necessary,
for appearance' sake, that he should keep strictly to his
hiding-place, he does not seem to have incurred any real
danger. The municipal authorities of Amsterdam had
too great a horror of Popery and too much sympathy with
liberty to show any marked zeal in carrying out the wishes
of the English king; nor does the Prince of Orange himself appear to have been very eager to hunt out the fugi-
tives, provided they went through the decent ceremony of
concealing themselves from the ministers of justice. To

Locke the confinement was doubtless irksome; but he was solaced by the visits of his friends, especially of Limborch, and the monotony of his solitude was broken by a visit of a few weeks to Cleve. Here, however, he does not appear to have felt so safe as at Amsterdam; and, consequently, he soon returned to his old quarters, assuming the name of Dr. Van der Linden, as at Cleve he had assumed that of Lamy. Meanwhile, two of his friends in England— William Penn, the celebrated Quaker, and the Earl of Pembroke, to whom he afterwards dedicated the *Essay*— were moving the king for a pardon. The latter, writing to Locke on the 20th of August, informs him that the king "bid me write to you to come over; I told him I would then bring you to kiss his hand, and he was fully satisfied I should." Locke, however, appears to have had little confidence in the king's sincerity, and, perhaps, no desire to compromise any political action that might be open to him in the future by making formal submission to a monarch who was tolerably certain to work out his own ruin. He still remained in concealment, and replied that, "having been guilty of no crime, he had no occasion for a pardon." But in May, 1686, all fear of arrest was removed by the appearance of a new proclamation of the States-General, in which his name was not included, and henceforth he was enabled to move about with perfect freedom.

The name of Limborch, one of the friends whom Locke made in Holland, has already been mentioned. A long series of letters which passed between them, beginning with Locke's arrival at Cleve in September, 1685, and ending only a few weeks before his death, is still extant, though some are still unpublished. This correspondence is interesting, not only as throwing light on Locke's pur-

suits, but also as affording a free expression of his theological opinions. Thus, in a letter written to Limborch soon
after his arrival at Cleve, with reference to a work recently
published by Le Clerc, he acknowledges his perplexities
respecting the plenary inspiration of the Bible. " If all
things which are contained in the sacred books are equally
to be regarded as inspired, without any distinctions, then
we give philosophers a great handle for doubting of our
faith and sincerity. If, on the contrary, some things are
to be regarded as purely human, how shall we establish
the divine authority of the Scriptures, without which the
Christian religion will fall to the ground ?   What shall
be our criterion ?   Where shall we draw the line ?"   He
applies to Limborch for help.   " For many things which
occur in the canonical books, long before I read this treatise, have made me anxious and doubtful, and I shall
be most grateful if you could remove my scruples." From
the character of his theological writings, composed during
the latter years of his life, it would appear that these
scruples were afterwards either removed or set aside.

With Le Clerc (Joannes Clericus) himself Locke first
became personally acquainted after his return to Amsterdam in the winter of 1685-6. Le Clerc was still young,
having been born at Geneva in 1657, but he had already
acquired considerable reputation both as a philosopher
and as a theologian. As a philosopher, he had at first
embraced the doctrines of Descartes, but, in after-life, he
leaned rather to those views which, a few years after the
time of which I am writing, became famous by the publication of Locke's *Essay*. As a divine, his theology was
liberal and critical beyond even that of the Remonstrant
School. He questioned the Mosaic authorship of the
Pentateuch, regarded some of the books of the Old Testa-

E

ment as of purely human origin, and, in his treatment of
the miracles and of Christian doctrine, rationalized so far
as to expose himself to the charge of Socinianism, though
he himself warmly repudiated the imputation. In literary
activity and enterprise, he yielded to no other author of
the age. Such a man, full of energy and of novel views,
ready to entertain and discuss any question of interest in
theology, criticism, or philosophy, must have been peculiarly acceptable to an exile like Locke, whose mind was
now engaged with just the same problems that were occupying Le Clerc. The intimacy between the two students,
though never so affectionate as that between Locke and
Limborch, soon became a close one. Though widely
separated in age, and though differing, probably, in many
of their specific opinions, they were conscious that they
were travelling the same road ; a way then little fre-
quented ; the way which led from the received tenets of
the churches and the schools to the arena of free inquiry
and impartial investigation.

In the winter of 1685-6, Locke, while still hiding in
Dr. Veen's house, employed himself in writing the famous
Epistola de Tolerantia, addressed to Limborch. This
tract was not, however, published till 1689, when it was
almost immediately translated into English, Dutch, and
French. Of the opinions expressed in this and the other
letters on Toleration I shall have occasion to speak hereafter, when describing Locke's theological views. It must
be recollected that, though now in his fifty-fourth year, he
had as yet published nothing of any importance. He had
indeed for several years been slowly putting together the
materials for many books ; but it is possible that his natural modesty, together with what seems to have been an
excessive prudence, might have prevented him from giving

any of his thoughts to the world, at least during his life-time, had it not been for the fortunate circumstances which brought him into contact with Le Clerc. At the time when the two friends were introduced to one another, Le Clerc was projecting the *Bibliothèque Universelle*, one of the earliest literary and scientific reviews, and to this Locke soon became a constant contributor. In the July number of 1686 appears his method of a Common-place Book, under the title, *Méthode Nouvelle de dresser des Recueils*. The ice was now broken, and from this time onwards we shall find his publications follow one another in rapid succession.

In September, 1686, Locke moved again to Utrecht, intending, apparently, to make a prolonged residence there; but in December, for some mysterious reason with which we are not acquainted, though connected in all probability with English politics, he was threatened with expulsion from the city, and was obliged to return to Amsterdam. It seems, from his correspondence with Limborch, that he did not wish this expulsion to be talked about. At the same time, he accepted stoically the inconveniences to which it put him. "These are the sports of fortune, or rather the ordinary chances of human life, which come as naturally as wind and rain to travellers." At Amsterdam he remained for two months as the guest of his old friend, Dr. Guenellon, and then removed to Rotterdam, where, with occasional breaks, he resided during the rest of his stay in Holland. This removal was undoubtedly con-nected with the turn which English politics were now taking at the Dutch Court. Monmouth being now out of the way, the only quarter to which those who were weary of the Stuart despotism could look for redress was the House of Orange. Secret negotiations were at this time

going on with the Prince and Princess, and there can
be no doubt that Locke was taking an active share in
the schemes that were in preparation. Rotterdam was
within a short distance of the Hague, and also a convenient place for carrying on a correspondence with England as well as for meeting the Englishmen who landed
in Holland. As soon as Locke arrived at Rotterdam his
hands seem to have been tolerably full of political business. Writing to Limborch in February, 1686-7, he says,
" To politics I gave but little thought at Amsterdam ; here
I cannot pay much attention to literature." Mr. Fox Bourne
conjectures that it was through Lord Mordaunt, afterwards Earl of Peterborough, who shortly before this
time had taken up his residence in Holland, that Locke
was brought into personal relations with the Prince and
Princess. Any way, these relations gradually ripened into
friendship, and a mutual feeling of respect and admiration
seems soon to have grown up between him and the royal
couple.

While at Rotterdam, Locke resided with Benjamin
Furly, an English Quaker, who was a merchant of considerable wealth and a great book-collector. At Furly's
death in 1714, the sale-catalogue of his books occupied
nearly 400 pages. Locke was thus at no loss for the
instruments of his trade, and, notwithstanding his pre-
occupation in politics, he seems to have been working
with fair assiduity at the *Essay* and on other literary subjects. In the number of the *Bibliothèque Universelle* for
January, 1687-8, appeared an abstract of the *Essay*, translated into French by Le Clerc, from a manuscript written
by Locke, which is still extant. The epitome was announced as communicated by Monsieur Locke, and a note
was appended inviting criticisms, if anything false, obscure,

or defective were remarked in the system.   After the
review had appeared, separate copies of the epitome were
struck off, and the opuscule, with a short dedication to
the Earl of Pembroke, was published in a separate form.
Locke went to Amsterdam for the purpose of superintend-
ing the printing of the epitome, and appears to have been
sorely tried by the "drunken" and "lying" workmen,
who, however, were all "good Christians," "orthodox
believers," and "marked for salvation by the distinguishing L that stands on their door-posts, or the funeral sermon
that they may have for a passport if they will go to the
charge of it."   On the 29th of February he returned to
Furly's house, where he seems to have lived in great
comfort, and on most intimate and affectionate terms with
the family.   One of the sons, a little boy of four or five
years old, named Arent, was a special favourite, and is
playfully alluded to in the letters to Furly as "my little
friend!"   Kindness to children seems always to have been
one of Locke's characteristics, as it is of all men of simple
manners and warm hearts.

   It was on the 1st of November, 1688, that William of
Orange set out on his expedition to England.   Locke still
remained in Holland, and appears to have had frequent
interviews with the Princess Mary, who was waiting till
she could with safety join her husband.   At last the word
was given from England, and, after being detained for
some time by unfavourable weather, the royal party,
accompanied by Locke and Lady Mordaunt, left the Hague
on the 11th of February, 1688-9.   They arrived at
Greenwich on the following day.   It was with mixed
feelings that Locke took leave of the country where he had
been entertained so long, and where he had formed so many
warm and congenial friendships.   Writing to Limborch

shortly before his departure, he says : "There are many
considerations which urge me not to miss this opportunity
of sailing : the expectation of my friends ; my private
affairs, which have now been long neglected ; the number
of pirates in the channel; and the charge of the noble lady
(Lady Mordaunt) with whom I am about to travel.   But
I trust that you will believe me when I say that I have
found here another country, and I might almost say other
relations ; for all that is dearest in that expression—good-
will, love, kindness—bonds that are stronger than blood—
I have experienced amongst you.   It is owing to this
fellow-feeling, which has always been shown to me by your
countrymen, that, though absent from my own people and
exposed to every kind of trouble, I have never yet felt sick
at heart." [1]   Still, it must have been with a thrill of delight
that, after an absence of more than five years, he once
more stepped on the shores of his native land, and felt
that a new era of liberty and glory had dawned for her.

About a week after his arrival in England, Locke was
offered, through Lord Mordaunt, the post of ambassador
to Frederick the First, Elector of Brandenburg.   The letter
to Lord Mordaunt, in which he declines the post, shows
the feeble condition in which, notwithstanding all his pre-
cautions, his health still continued.   "It is the most
touching displeasure I have ever received from that weak
and broken constitution of my health, which has so long
threatened my life, that it now affords me not a body
suitable to my mind in so desirable an occasion of serving
his Majesty. . . . . What shall a man do in the necessity
of application and variety of attendance on business who
sometimes, after a little motion, has not breath to speak,

---

[1] It should be mentioned, perhaps, that the correspondence between Locke and Limborch is in Latin.

and cannot borrow an hour or two of watching from the night without repaying it with a great waste of time the next day?" But there was another reason, besides his health, why he could not accept a mission to the Court of Brandenburg. "If I have reason to apprehend the cold air of the country, there is yet another thing in it as inconsistent with my constitution, and that is their warm drinking." It was true that he might oppose obstinate refusal, but then that would be to take more care of his own health than of the king's business. "It is no small matter in such stations to be acceptable to the people one has to do with, in being able to accommodate one's self to their fashions; and I imagine, whatever I may do there myself, the knowing what others are doing is at least one half of my business, and I know no such rack in the world to draw out men's thoughts as a well-managed bottle. If, therefore, it were fit for me to advise in this case, I should think it more for the king's interest to send a man of equal parts, that could drink his share, than the soberest man in the kingdom." But, though Locke shrank from this post, the importance of which could hardly be exaggerated, for Frederick was the ally on whom William most confided in his opposition to Louis the Fourteenth, he was ready to place his services at the disposal of the Government for domestic work. "If there be anything wherein I may flatter myself I have attained any degree of capacity to serve his Majesty, it is in some little knowledge I perhaps may have in the constitutions of my country, the temper of my countrymen, and the divisions amongst them, whereby I persuade myself I may be more useful to him at home, though I cannot but see that such an employment would be of greater advantage to myself abroad, would but my health assent to it." The disin-

terested patriotism of this letter was only of a piece with
the whole of Locke's political life. He was next offered
the embassy to Vienna, and, in fact, invited to name any
diplomatic appointment which he would be prepared to
accept; but he regarded his health as an insuperable bar
to work of this kind at so critical a time in the history of
Europe. Having declined all foreign employment, he was
now named a Commissioner of Appeals, an office with
small emolument and not much work, which he appears
to have retained during the remainder of his life. This
office seems to have been given to him partly as a com-
pensation for the arrears of salary due under the late
Government; for, with an exhausted exchequer, it was
impossible to satisfy such claims by immediate payment.

Locke's health suffered considerably by his return to
London. Writing to Limborch shortly after his arrival,
and complaining of the worry caused him by the pressure
of private affairs and public business, the climax of all his
grievances, we are hardly surprised to find, is the injury
to his health "from the pestilent smoke of this city"
(*Malignus hujus urbis fumus*). Amongst the public affairs
which claimed his attention, the foremost, doubtless, was
the attempt then being made to widen the basis of the
National Church by a measure of comprehension, as well
as to relieve of civil disabilities the more extreme or
scrupulous of the sectaries by what was called a measure
of indulgence or toleration. Locke, of course, with his
friend Lord Mordaunt, took the most liberal side open to
him as respects these measures ; but he complains that the
episcopal clergy were unfavourable to these as well as to
other reforms, whether to their own advantage and that of
the State it was for them to consider. Unfortunately
both for the Church and nation, the issue of the religious

struggles which were carried on at the beginning of
William's reign was, on the whole, in favour of the less
tolerant party. The Comprehension Bill, after being
violently attacked and languidly defended, was dropped
altogether. The Toleration Bill, though passed by pretty
general consent, and affording a considerable measure of
relief on the existing law, was entirely of the nature of a
compromise, and what we should now note as most
remarkable in it is the number of its provisos and exceptions. No relief was granted to the believer in transubstantiation or the disbeliever in the Trinity. No dissenting
minister, moreover, was allowed to exercise his vocation
unless he subscribed thirty four out of the Thirty-nine
Articles, together with the greater part of two others.
The Quakers had to make a special declaration of belief in
the Holy Trinity and in the Divine inspiration of the
Scriptures. The measure of toleration which Locke would
have been prepared to grant, it need hardly be said, far
exceeded that which was accorded by the Act. Speaking
of the law recently passed in a letter to Limborch on the
6th of June, he uses apologetic language. "Toleration has
indeed been granted, but not with that latitude which
you and men like you, true Christians without ambition
or envy, would desire. But it is something to have got
thus far. On these beginnings I hope are laid the foundations of liberty and peace on which the Church of
Christ will hereafter be established." In a subsequent
letter, speaking again of the same law, he says, "People
will always differ from one another about religion, and
carry on constant strife and war, until the right of every
one to perfect liberty in these matters is conceded, and
they can be united in one body by a bond of mutual
charity." If there be any truth in the tradition to which

Lord King alludes, that Locke himself negotiated the
terms of the Toleration Act, he must have regarded it
simply as an instalment of religious liberty, the utmost
that could be procured under the circumstances, and an
earnest of better things to come.

On William's accession to the throne, one only of the
English Sees was vacant, the Bishopric of Salisbury.   To
this he nominated the famous Gilbert Burnet, who had
been one of his advisers in Holland.   Locke, in one of his
letters to Limborch, tells a rather malicious story of the
new prelate.   When he paid his first visit to the king
after his consecration, his Majesty observed that his hat
was a good deal larger than usual, and asked him what
was the object of so very much brim.   The bishop replied
that it was the shape suitable to his dignity.   " I hope,"
answered the king, " that the hat won't turn your head."

The topic that most interested Locke probably at this
time, next to the political regeneration of his country, was
the approaching publication of the *Essay*.   The work
must have been finished, or all but finished, when he left
Holland.   In May, 1689, he wrote the dedication to the
Earl of Pembroke, and the printing commenced shortly
afterwards.   The proof-sheets were sent to Le Clerc.   As
before at Amsterdam, the printers appear to have caused
him some trouble, but the book was in the booksellers'
shops early in 1690.   It is a fine folio, " printed by Eliz.
Holt for Thomas Basset at the George in Fleet Street,
near St. Dunstan's Church."   Locke received 30*l*. for the
copyright.   But when we remember that Milton only
lived to receive 10*l*. for *Paradise Lost*, we cannot feel
much surprise at Locke's rate of payment.   The days
when authorship was to become a lucrative profession
were still far distant in England.

Previously to the publication of the *Essay*, in the spring of 1689, the *Epistola de Tolerantia* had appeared at Gouda, in Holland; but it was published anonymously, and apparently without Locke's knowledge, the responsibility of giving it to the world being undertaken by Limborch, to whom it had been addressed. On the title-page are some mysterious letters, the invention, probably, of Limborch : " Epistola de Tolerantia ad Clarissimum Virum T. A. R. P. T. O. L. A. Scripta a P. A. P. O. I. L. A." These being interpreted, are, " Theologiæ Apud Remonstrantes Professorem, Tyrannidis Osorem, Limborchium Amstelodamensem ;" and "Pacis Amico, Persecutionis Osore, Joanne Lockio Anglo." Dutch and French translations were issued almost immediately, and the book at once created considerable discussion on the Continent; but it does not at the first appear to have excited much attention in England. Locke himself was for some time unable to obtain a copy. In the course of the year, however, it was translated into English by one William Popple, an Unitarian merchant residing in London. In the preface the translator, alluding to recent legislation, says, " We have need of more generous remedies than what have yet been made use of in our distemper. It is neither declarations of indulgence nor acts of comprehension, such as have as yet been practised or projected amongst us, that can do the work. Absolute liberty, just and true liberty, equal and impartial liberty, is the thing that we stand in need of."

Locke affords a curious instance of a man who, having carefully shunned publication up to a late period of life, then gave forth a series of works in rapid succession. It would seem as if he had long mistrusted his own powers, or as if he had doubted of the expediency of at once

seeking a wide circulation for his views, but that, having
once ventured to reveal himself to the public, he was
emboldened, if not impelled, to proceed.   Early in 1690,
there appeared not only the *Essay*, but also the *Two
Treatises of Government*.   These were published anonymously, but it must soon have been known that Locke was
their author.   For reasons which I have given in
another chapter, the former of the two treatises, which is
a criticism of Sir Robert Filmer's *Patriarcha*, seems to
have been written between 1680 and 1685, the latter
during the concluding period of Locke's stay in Holland,
while the English Revolution was being prepared and
consummated.

The translation of the Epistle on Toleration soon provoked a lively controversy.   To one answer, that by Jonas
Proast, Locke replied in a *Second Letter concerning
Toleration*, signed by Philanthropus, and dated May 27th,
1690.   Proast, as the manner is in such controversies,
replied again, and Locke wrote a *Third Letter for
Toleration*, again signed Philanthropus, and dated June
20, 1692.   After many years' silence, Proast wrote a
rejoinder in 1704, and to this Locke replied in the
Fourth Letter for Toleration, which, however, he did
not live to publish, or, indeed, to complete.   It appeared
amongst his Posthumous Works.   These Letters on Toleration doubtless exercised great influence in their day, and
probably contributed, in large measure, to bring about the
more enlightened views on this subject which in this
country, at least, are now all but universal.

The authorship of the Letters on Toleration, though it
could hardly fail to be pretty generally known, was first
distinctly acknowledged by Locke in the codicil to his
will.   Limborch, on being hard pressed, had divulged it,

in the spring of 1690, to Guenellon and Veen, but they appear, contrary to what generally happens in such cases, to have kept the secret to themselves. Locke, however, was much irritated at the indiscretion of Limborch, and, for once, wrote him an angry letter. " If you had entrusted me with a secret of this kind, I would not have divulged it to relation, or friend, or any mortal being, under any circumstances whatsoever. You do not know the trouble into which you have brought me." It is not easy to see why Locke should have felt so disquieted at the prospect of his authorship being discovered, but it may be that he hoped to bring about some extension of the limits of the Toleration Act which had been passed in the preceding year, and that he feared that his hands might be tied by the discovery that he entertained what, at that time, would be regarded as such extreme views ; or it may have been simply that he was afraid, if his authorship were once acknowledged, of being dragged into a long and irksome controversy with the bigots of the various ecclesiastical parties, which were then endeavouring to maintain or recover their ascendancy.

CHAPTER V.

SHORTLY after Locke returned to England, he settled down in lodgings in the neighbourhood of what is now called Cannon Row, Westminster. But the fogs and smoke of London then, as now, were not favourable to persons of delicate health, and he seems to have been glad of any opportunity of breathing the country air. Amongst his places of resort were Parson's Green, the suburban residence of Lord Mordaunt, now Earl of Monmouth, and Oates, a manor-house, in the parish of High Laver, in Essex, the seat of Sir Francis and Lady Masham, situated in a pleasant pastoral country, about twenty miles from London. Lady Masham had become known to him as Damaris Cudworth, before his retreat to Holland, and it is plain that from the first she had excited his admiration and esteem. She was the daughter of Dr. Ralph Cudworth, Master of Christ's College, Cambridge, author of *The True Intellectual System of the Universe*, and of a posthumous work, still better known, *A Treatise concerning Eternal and Immutable Morality*. The close connexion which, in the latter years of his life, subsisted between Locke, the foremost name amongst the empirical philosophers of modern times, and the daughter of Cudworth, the most uncompromising of the *a priori* moralists and philosophers of the seventeenth century, may be regarded as one of the ironies of literary history. Damaris Cudworth, inheriting her father's tastes, took great interest in learning of all kinds, and specially in philosophy and theology. There was one point of community between her father and Locke, besides their common pursuits, namely, the wide and philosophical view which they both took of theological controversies. Cudworth belonged to the small but learned and refined group of Cambridge Platonists or Latitudinarians, as they were called, which also numbered Henry More, John Smith, Culverwell, and Whichcote. Liberal and tolerant Churchmanship in those days, when it was so rare, was probably a much closer bond of union than it is now, and the associations which she had formed with her father's liberal, philosophical, and devout spirit must have helped to endear Locke to the daughter of Dr. Cudworth. During Locke's absence from England, Damaris Cudworth had married, as his second wife, Sir Francis Masham, an amiable and hospitable country gentleman, who seems to have occupied a prominent position in his county. With them lived Mrs. Cudworth, the widow of Dr. Cudworth, one little son, Francis, and a daughter by the former marriage, Esther, who was about fourteen when Locke commenced his visits to the family. From the first he seems to have had some idea of settling down at Oates, "making trial of the air of the place," than which, as Lady Masham tells us, "he thought none would be more suitable to him." After a very severe illness in the autumn of 1690, he spent several months with the Mashams, and appears then to have formed a more definite plan of making Oates his home. But, though his hospitable friends gave him every assurance of a constant welcome, he would only consent to regard it as a per-

manent residence on his own terms, which were that he
should pay his share of the household expenses. With
true kindness and courtesy, Sir Francis and Lady
Masham, at last, in the spring of 1691, agreed to this
arrangement, and "Mr. Locke then," says Lady Masham,
"believed himself at home with us, and resolved, if it
pleased God, here to end his days—as he did." Devoted
and sympathetic friends, a pleasant residence, freedom
from domestic or pecuniary cares, and the pure fresh air of
the country seem to have afforded him all the enjoyment
and leisure which we could have wished for him. After
having had more than his share of the storms of life, he
had at last found a quiet and pleasant haven wherein to
enjoy the calm and sunshine of his declining years.
Occasionally, and especially during the summer, he visited
London, where, at first, he retained his old chambers at
Westminster, moving afterwards to Lincoln's Inn Fields.
But Oates was now his home, and it continued to be so to
the end of his life.

Locke was always an attached friend, and we have seen
already how many warm friendships he had formed in
youth and middle age. At the present time, besides
Limborch, Le Clerc, Lord Monmouth, and the Mashams,
we may mention among his more intimate friends, Lord
Pembroke, the young Lord Ashley, Somers, Boyle, and
Newton. Lord Pembroke (to whom the *Essay* is dedicated in what we should now regard as a tone of over-
wrought compliment) opened his town house for weekly
meetings in which, instead of political and personal
gossip, things of the mind were discussed. These con-
versations, " undisturbed by such as could not bear a part
in the best entertainment of rational minds, free discourse
concerning useful truths," were a source of great enjoy-

ment to Locke during his London residence. It was
through his introduction that Lord Pembroke, when sent
on a special mission to the Hague, made the acquaintance, which afterwards ripened into friendship, of Limborch and Le Clerc.

The correspondence between Locke and Limborch,
while Lord Pembroke was in Holland, reveals to us the
curious fact that there was no organized carrying trade between England and Holland at that time.   On returning,
the Earl, or his Secretary, was commissioned to bring
back a pound of tea and copies of the *Acta Eruditorum*.
The tea must be had at any price.   " I want the best
tea," Locke writes to Limborch, " even if it costs forty
florins a pound ; only you must be quick, or we shall lose
this opportunity, and I doubt whether we shall have
another."   The price that he was ready to pay for a
pound of tea would be about 9*l*. at the present value of
money.   But tea at that time was regarded rather as a
medicine than a beverage.

Young Lord Ashley, it will be recollected, had, like his
father, been under the charge of Locke, when a child.
After being at school for some years at Winchester, and
spending some time in travelling on the Continent, he
was now again in London, living in his father's house at
Chelsea.   It is plain that the young philosopher saw a
good deal of his " foster-father," as he called him, and
they must often have discussed together the questions
which were so interesting to them both.   Ashley, moreover, who was already beginning to solve the problems of
philosophy in his own way, addressed a number of letters
to Locke, freely, but courteously and good-humouredly,
criticizing his master's views.

Sir John Somers, now Solicitor-General, and succes-

F

sively Attorney-General, Lord Keeper of the Great Seal, and Lord Chancellor, with the title of Lord Somers, had been known to Locke before his retirement to Holland. They were both of them attached to the Shaftesbury connexion, and, hence, though Somers was nearly twenty years the junior, they had probably already seen a good deal of each other when William ascended the throne. On Locke's return to England, he found Somers a member of the Convention Parliament. The younger man, both when he was a rising barrister and a successful minister, seems frequently to have consulted the elder one, and Locke's principles of government, finance, and toleration, must often have exerted a considerable influence both on his speeches and his measures. Nor had Locke any reason to be ashamed of his teaching. "Lord Somers," says Horace Walpole, "was one of those divine men who, like a chapel in a palace, remain unprofaned, while all the rest is tyranny, corruption, and folly." It was, perhaps, through Somers that Locke made the acquaintance of another great and wise statesman, Charles Montague, subsequently Lord Halifax, with whom, at least during the later years of his life, he had much political connexion, and by whom he was frequently called into counsel.

The acquaintance between Locke and Newton, of whom Newton was the junior by more than ten years, most probably began before Locke's departure to Holland. Both had then for some time been members of the Royal Society, and both were friends of Boyle. The first positive evidence, however, that we have of their relations is afforded by a paper, entitled "A Demonstration that the Planets, by their gravity towards the Sun, may move in Eclipses," and endorsed in Locke's handwriting, "Mr. Newton, March, 1689." In the summer or autumn of the same year, probably, was written the epistle to the reader, prefixed to the *Essay*. In that occurs the following passage, expressing no doubt Locke's genuine opinion of the great writers whom he names :—"The Commonwealth of learning is not at this time without master-builders, whose mighty designs in advancing the sciences will leave lasting monuments to the admiration of posterity ; but every one must not hope to be a Boyle or a Sydenham, and in an age that produces such masters as the great Huygenius and the incomparable Mr. Newton, with some other of that strain, tis ambition enough to be employed as an under-labourer in clearing ground a little, and removing some of the rubbish that lies in the way to knowledge." Locke interested himself long and warmly in attempting to obtain for Newton some lucrative appointment in London.   Newton's letters occasionally betray querulousness, but there can be no reason to suppose that Locke at all flagged in his efforts, and, ultimately, with the assistance of Lord Monmouth, Lord Halifax, and others, they proved successful.   Newton was, in course of time, appointed Warden, and then Master of the Mint.   In January, 1690-1, the philosopher and the mathematician met at Oates.   Their conversation there probably turned chiefly on theological topics, as was the case with most of their correspondence afterwards.   Newton was greatly interested not only in theological speculation, but in the intepretation of prophecy and Biblical criticism, on both of which subjects works by him are extant.   In 1690 he wrote a manuscript letter to Locke, entitled, "An Historical Account of Two Notable Corruptions of Scripture in a Letter to a Friend," the texts criticized being 1 John v. 7, and 1 Timothy iii. 16.   The corruption of the former of these texts is now almost univer-

sally, and that of the latter very generally, acknowledged,
but so jealous of orthodoxy, in respect of anything which
seemed to affect the doctrine of the Trinity, was public
opinion at that time that Newton did not dare to publish
the pamphlet. Locke, who was meditating a visit to
Holland, was, by Newton's wish, to have taken it over
with him, and to have had it translated into French, and
published anonymously. But the intended visit fell
through, and Locke sent the manuscript over to Le Clerc.
So timid, however, was Newton that he now tried to
recall it. "Let me entreat you," he writes to Locke, "'to
stop the translation and impression of the papers as soon
as you can, for I desire to suppress them." Le Clerc
thought more nobly and more justly that " one ought to
risk a little in order to be of service to those honest folk
who err only through ignorance, and who, if they get a
chance, would gladly be disabused of their false notions."
The letter was not published till after its author's death,
and at first it appeared only in an imperfect form. In
Bishop Horsley's edition of Newton it is printed complete. Newton's unpublished writings leave no doubt
that he did not accept the orthodox doctrine of the
Trinity, and it may have been his consciousness of this
fact which made him so afraid of being known to be the
author of what was merely a critical exercitation. But
we must recollect that at this time Biblical criticism was
unfamiliar to the majority of divines, and that to question
the authenticity of a text was generally regarded as identical with doubting the doctrine which it was supposed to
illustrate. One of the other subjects on which Locke and
Newton corresponded was a parcel of red earth which had
been left by Boyle, who died on Dec. 30, 1691, to Locke
and his other literary executors, with directions for turn-

ing it into gold. Locke seems to have had some faith in
the alchemistic process, but it is plain that Newton had
none. He was satisfied that "mercury, by this recipe,
might be brought to change its colours and properties, but
not that gold might be multiplied thereby." Some workmen of whom he had heard as practising the recipe had
been forced to other means of living, a proof that the
multiplication of gold did not succeed as a profession.
Occasionally, owing to Newton's nervous and irritable
temper, which at one time threatened to settle down into
a fixed melancholy, there seems to have been some mis-
understanding of Locke on his part, but it is satisfactory
to know that the two greatest literary men of their age in
England, if not in Europe, lived, almost without inter-
ruption, in friendly and even intimate relations with each
other.

The close intercourse between Boyle and Locke, which
dated from their Oxford days, seems to have been
kept up till the time of Boyle's death. Locke made
a special journey to London to visit him on his death-
bed, and was, as we have seen, left one of his literary
executors. The editing of Boyle's *General History of
the Air* had already been committed to Locke, and
seems to have occupied much of his time during the
year 1691.

Of Locke's less-known friends, Dr. David Thomas must
have died between 1687, when there is a letter from him
to Locke, and 1700, when Locke speaks of having out-
lived him. Sir James Tyrrell, another old college friend,
usually spoken of in Locke's correspondence as Musidore,
was in communication with him as late as April, 1704,
the year of his death. He had, as already stated, been
present at the "meeting of five or six friends" in Locke's

chamber, which first suggested the composition of the *Essay*.

Edward Clarke, of Chipley, near Taunton, was another friend of old standing. He was elected member for Taunton in King William's second parliament, and from that time forward resided much in London. This circumstance probably deepened the intimacy between the two friends ; at all events, during the remainder of Locke's life they are constantly associated. Locke advised Clarke as to the education of his children, one of whom, Betty, a little girl now about ten years old, seems to have been regarded by him with peculiar affection ; in his letters he constantly speaks of her as " Mrs. Locke" and his " wife." The playful banter with which Locke treated his child friends affords unmistakeable evidence of the kindness and simplicity of his heart.

William Molyneux, who for many years represented the University of Dublin in the Irish parliament, referred to in the second edition of the *Essay* as "that very ingenious and studious promoter of real knowledge, the worthy and learned Mr. Molyneux," "this thinking gentleman whom, though I have never had the happiness to see, I am proud to call my friend," first became acquainted with Locke in 1692. In his *Dioptrica Nova*, published in that year, he had paid Locke a graceful, if not an exaggerated, compliment. " To none do we owe, for a greater advancement in this part of philosophy," he said, speaking of logic, " than to the incomparable Mr. Locke, who hath rectified more received mistakes, and delivered more profound truths, established on experience and observation, for the direction of man's mind in the prosecution of knowledge, which I think may be properly termed logic, than are to be met with in all the volumes of the ancients. He has clearly overthrown all those metaphysical whimsies which infected men's brains with a spice of madness, whereby they feigned a knowledge where they had none, by making a noise with sounds without clear and distinct significations." Locke was pleased with the compliment, and a letter acknowledging the receipt of Molyneux's book was the beginning of a long correspondence between them, which ended only with the early death of Molyneux, at the age of forty-two, in 1698. For nearly six years the friends, though in constant correspondence, had never seen each other, Molyneux residing in Dublin, and suffering, like Locke, from feeble health, which prevented him from crossing the channel. But the feeling of affection seems soon to have become as intense, notwithstanding Aristotle's dictum that personal intercourse is essential to the continuance of friendship, as if they had lived together all their lives. In his second letter to Molyneux, dated September 20, 1692, Locke says :—" You must expect to have me live with you hereafter, with all the liberty and assurance of a settled friendship. For meeting with but few men in the world whose acquaintance I find much reason to covet, I make more than ordinary haste into the familiarity of a rational inquirer after and lover of truth, whenever I can light on any such. There are beauties of the mind as well as of the body, that take and prevail at first sight ; and, wherever I have met with this, I have readily surrendered myself, and have never yet been deceived in my expectation." Molyneux had thought of coming over to England on a visit to Locke in the summer of 1694. Locke, in a letter written in the following spring, after deprecating the risks to which his journey might expose him, adds :— " And yet, if I may confess my secret thoughts, there is not anything which I would not give, that some other unavoidable occasion would draw you into England. A rational, free-minded man, tied to nothing but truth, is so rare a thing that I almost worship such a friend ; but, when friendship is joined to it, and these are brought into a free conversation, where they meet and can be together, what is there can have equal charms ? I cannot but exceedingly wish for that happy day when I may see a man I have so often longed to have in my embraces. . . . . You cannot think how often I regret the distance that is between us ; I envy Dublin for what I every day want in London." In a subsequent letter, written in 1695, he writes :—" I cannot complain that I have not my share of friends of all ranks, and such, whose interest, assistance, affection, and opinions too, in fit cases, I can rely on. But methinks, for all this, there is one place vacant that I know nobody would so well fill as yourself ; I want one near me to talk freely with " de quolibet ente," to propose to the extravagancies that rise in my mind ; one with whom I would debate several doubts and questions to see what was in them." Thomas Molyneux, the brother of William, a physician practising in Dublin, had met Locke during his stay in Holland. They shared a common admiration for Sydenham, and the correspondence with William Molyneux revived their friendship, though it never attained to nearly the same proportions as that between Locke and the other brother. A passage on what may be called the Logic of Medicine, in one of Locke's letters to Thomas Molyneux, is worth quoting :—" What we know of the works of nature, especially in the constitution of health and the operations of our own bodies, is only by the sensible effects, but not by any certainty we can have of the tools she uses or the ways she walks by. So that there is nothing left for a physician to do but to observe well, and so, by analogy, argue to like cases, and thence make to himself rules of practice."

November 7, 1691, is the date of the dedication of the Tract entitled, " Some considerations on the Lowering of. Interest and Raising the Value of Money in a letter sent to a Member of Parliament, 1691." This letter was published anonymously in the following year. The member of Parliament was undoubtedly Sir John Somers, who had "put" the author "upon looking out his old papers concerning the reducing of interest to 4 per cent., which had so long," nearly twenty years, "lain by, forgotten." The time to which Locke refers must be the year 1672, when the Exchequer was closed, that is to say, all payments to the public creditors suspended for a year, and the interest on the Bankers' advances reduced to six per cent. This nefarious act of spoliation, which caused wide-spread ruin and distress, was devised while Shaftesbury was Chancellor of the Exchequer, but the main blame in the transaction probably attaches to Clifford. "The notions concerning coinage," which are embodied in the second division of the pamphlet, had been put into writing and apparently shown to Somers about twelve months before the date of the letter. On the occasion and contents of this pamphlet, as well as of Locke's other tracts on Finance, I shall have an opportunity of speaking in subsequent chapters.

Many of my readers will sympathize with Locke in his complaints of the waste of his time during this autumn. Writing to Limborch on Nov. 14, he says, "I know not how it is, but the pressure of other people's business has left me no time or leisure for my own affairs. Do not suppose

that I mean public business. I have neither health, nor
strength, nor knowledge enough to attend to that. And
when I ask myself what has so hampered and occupied
me during the last three months, it seems as if a sort of
spell had been thrown on me, so that I have got entangled
first in one business and then in another, without being
able to avoid it, or, in fact, to foresee what was coming."
Locke was pre-eminently a good-natured man, and, like
many other men before and since, he had to pay the
penalty of good-nature by doing a vast amount of other
people's business, often probably with scant acknowledgment. One of the occupations in which he was engaged
may have been doctoring the household at Oates and
advising medically for his friends at a distance ; but in
business of this kind, though he may have grudged the time
it consumed, he seems always to have taken special delight.

In the summer of 1692 he spent a considerable time
in London. His main business there seems to have been
to see the *Third Letter on Toleration* through the press.
But he was now, as ever, ready to do work for his friends.
Thus he obtained for Limborch the permission to dedicate
the book which he had so long been preparing, the
Historia Inquisitionis, to Tillotson, then Archbishop of
Canterbury. Limborch evidently set great store on this
privilege. Of Tillotson, Locke seems to have entertained
a very high opinion ; which, indeed, was thoroughly well-
deserved. "In proportion to his renown and worth is
his modesty." Tillotson was not one of those liberal
Churchmen whom promotion makes timid, or cold to their
former friends. He was maligned by an unforgiving and
unscrupulous faction, more, perhaps, than any other man
of that age, but he always retained the courage of his
opinions.

Locke's health seems to have suffered much during the winter of 1692-3.   But he still occupied himself with literary work.   While in Holland, he had corresponded frequently with Clarke on the education of his children. Yielding to the solicitation of many of his friends, especially William Molyneux, he now reduced the letters to the form of a treatise, which was published in July, 1693, under the title, *Some Thoughts concerning Education.*   The dedication to Clarke bears date in the previous March, and is signed by Locke, though his name does not appear on the title-page.   The most serious work, however, in which he was now engaged, was the preparation of a second edition of the *Essay.*   The first edition seems to have been exhausted in the autumn of 1692. On the alterations and additions introduced into the second edition, there is an interesting correspondence with Molyneux, ranging from Sept. 20, 1692, to May 26, 1694, when the new edition, notwithstanding the "slowness of the press," was " printed and bound, and ready to be sent " to Locke's Dublin correspondent.   Besides suggestions in detail, such as those touching the questions of liberty and personal identity, Molyneux urged Locke to undertake a separate work on Ethics, a suggestion which for a time he entertained favourably, but which, owing partly, perhaps, to his idea that the principles and rules of morality ought to be presented in a demonstrative form, was never carried out.   Though he does not seem to have doubted that " morality might be demonstrably made out," yet whether he was able so to make it out was another question.   " Every one could not have demonstrated what Mr. Newton's book hath shown to be demonstrable."   He was, however, ready to employ the first leisure he could find that way.   But the treatise never proceeded beyond a few rough notes. Another reason assigned, at a later period, for not more seriously setting about this task was that " the Gospel contains so perfect a body of ethics, that reason may be excused for that inquiry, since she may find man's duty clearer and easier in revelation than in herself." This argument shows, at once, the sincerity of Locke's religious convictions, and the inadequate conception he had formed to himself of the grounds and nature of Moral Philosophy. Another suggestion made by Molyneux, was that, besides a second edition of the *Essay,* Locke should bring out, in accordance with the main lines of his philosophy, another work forming a complete compendium of logic and metaphysics for the use of University Students. No one can regret that the author of the *Essay* did not adopt this advice. Apropos of this suggestion, Molyneux tells Locke that Dr. Ashe, then Provost of Trinity College, Dublin, " was so wonderfully pleased and satisfied with the work, that he has ordered it to be read by the bachelors in the college, and strictly examines them in their progress therein." From that time onwards the *Essay* seems to have held its ground as a class-book at Dublin. The reception which it met with at first from the authorities of Locke's own University, as we shall see presently, was widely different. In May, 1694, the second edition was on sale, and was quickly exhausted. The third edition, which is simply a reprint of the second, appeared in the following year. One more edition, the fourth, dated 1700, but issued in the autumn of 1699, appeared during Locke's lifetime. In it there are important alterations and additions, including two new chapters, that on Enthusiasm, and the very important one, at the end of the second book, on the Association of Ideas. A Latin translation of the *Essay* by Richard

Burridge, an Irish Clergyman, was published at London, in 1701, and a French translation by Pierre Coste, who was a friend of Le Clerc, and had been acting for some time as tutor to young Frank Masham, at Amsterdam, in 1700. John Wynne, Fellow of Jesus College, Oxford, and subsequently Bishop of St. Asaph, published an abridgment for the use of University Students, in 1696. Wynne had a large number of pupils, and the compendium of Locke's philosophy appears to have obtained rapid circulation among the younger students in Oxford, only, however, as we shall soon see, to encounter the opposition of the authorities.

It is notable that all the important alterations and additions made in the second edition of the *Essay* were printed on separate slips and issued, without charge, to those who possessed the first. Sir James Tyrrell's copy of the first edition, with these slips pasted in, is in the British Museum, and that of William Molyneux in the Bodleian. In sending to Molyneux the second edition, Locke had also forwarded the slips to be pasted in the first, which would " help to make the book useful to any young man ;" but whether Molyneux gave the copy now in the Bodleian to "any young man," and, if so, who the fortunate young man was, we do not learn.

The first writer who had taken up his pen against Locke was John Norris, the amiable and celebrated Vicar of Bemerton, a religious and philosophical mystic, whose works are even still in repute. Norris was a disciple of Malebranche, and his attack seems to have had the effect of leading Locke to make a careful study of the theories of the French philosopher. The result was two tractates —one entitled, *Remarks upon some of Mr. Norris's Books;* the other, *An Examination of Père Malebranche's Opinion*

of seeing all things in God. The latter is much the more
considerable production of the two, and is mainly remarkable as showing that Locke saw clearly that the conclusions, subsequently drawn by Berkeley, must follow
from Malebranche's premises. Neither of these tracts
was published till after Locke's death. The reasons
assigned by him for not publishing his criticisms of Malebranche are characteristic : "I love not controversies, and
have a personal kindness for the author."

Locke's literary activity during the years 1689-95
appears excessive ; but we must recollect that he had
already accumulated a vast amount of material, and that,
during the latter part of that time at least, he must have
enjoyed considerable leisure in his country retirement. In
the early months of 1695 he was mainly occupied with a
new subject, the *Essay on the Reasonableness of Christianity as delivered in the Scriptures.* Though this work
was designed to establish the supernatural character of the
Christian revelation, and its importance to mankind, it by
no means satisfied the canons of a strict orthodoxy. Some
of the more mysterious and less intelligible doctrines of
the Christian Church, if not denied, were at least represented as unessential to saving faith. Hence it at once
provoked a bitter controversy. "The buz, the flutter, and
noise which was made, and the reports which were raised,"
says its author, "would have persuaded the world that it
subverted all morality, and was designed against the
Christian religion. I must confess, discussions of this
kind, which I met with, spread up and down, at first
amazed me ; knowing the sincerity of those thoughts
which persuaded me to publish it, not without some hope
of doing some service to decaying piety and mistaken and
slandered Christianity." The first assailant was John

Edwards, a former Fellow of St. John's College, Cambridge, who in a violent pamphlet, entitled *Thoughts concerning the Causes and Occasions of Atheism*, included the *Reasonableness of Christianity* in his attack, and insinuated that Locke was its author by affecting to disbelieve it. The book was described as "all over Socinianized," and a Socinian, if not an atheist, is, according to Edwards, "one that favours the cause of atheism." That there was much similarity between the apparent opinions of Locke and the doctrines of Faustus Socinus himself, though not of Socinus's more extreme followers, who were also popularly called Socinians, admits of no doubt. But the charge of favouring atheism can only have been brought against a man who regarded the existence of God as "the most obvious truth that reason discovers," and who appears never to have questioned the reality of supernatural intervention, from time to time, in the world's history, because it happened to be the roughest stone that could be found in the controversial wallet. Locke replied to Edwards with pardonable asperity in a tract entitled, *A Vindication of the Reasonableness of Christianity*. Edwards, of course, soon replied to the reply, and attacked Locke more violently than ever in his *Socinianism Unmasked*. No rejoinder followed, but the adversary was not to be let off on such easy terms. Another shot was fired, and *The Socinian Creed*, as venomous and more successful than the *Socinianism Unmasked*, provoked *A Second Vindication*. This lengthy pamphlet, far more elaborate than the first, must have occupied much of Locke's time. It did not appear till the spring of 1697. Edwards returned to the charge; but, fortunately, Locke had the wisdom and courage to refrain from carrying on the fight. Bitter as the feeling against

Locke must have been in many clerical circles at this time, there were not wanting, even amongst the clergy, those who sympathized with his views. Mr. Bolde, a Dorsetshire clergyman, came forward to defend him against Edwards. And Molyneux, writing on the 26th of September, 1696, says, "As to the *Reasonableness of Christianity*, I do not find but it is very well approved of here amongst candid, unprejudiced men, that dare speak their thoughts. I'll tell you what a very learned and ingenious prelate said to me on that occasion. I asked him whether he had read that book, and how he liked it. He told me very well; and that, if my friend Mr. Locke writ it, it was the best book he ever laboured at; 'but,' says he, 'if I should be known to think so, I should have my lawns torn from my shoulders.' But he knew my opinion aforehand, and was, therefore, the freer to commit his secret thoughts in that matter to me." We may not be disposed to think highly of the "very learned and ingenious prelate;" but the story shows, as indeed we know from other sources, to what a volume of opinion, both lay and clerical, on the expediency of presenting Christianity in a more "reasonable" and less mysterious and dogmatic form, Locke's treatise had given expression. Men were anxious to retain their beliefs in the supernatural order of events, but they were equally anxious to harmonize them with what they regarded as the necessities of reason. The current of "Rationalism" had set in.

It is satisfactory to know that, amidst all these controversial worries, which must have been most distasteful to a man of his habits and temper, Locke enjoyed the solace of pleasant companionship and domestic serenity. He was thoroughly at home at Oates, and Lord Monmouth and his other friends in and near town seem always to have been ready to accord him a hearty welcome, whenever he cared to pay them a visit. His little "wife," Betty Clarke, and her brother used occasionally to come on visits to him at the Mashams, and he seems to have taken great delight in the society of Esther Masham, who was now rapidly growing up to womanhood. "In raillery," wrote this lady many years afterwards, "he used to call me his Laudabridis, and I called him my John." The winters of 1694-5 and 1695-6 were unusually long and severe, and in both of them Locke appears to have been under apprehensions that his chronic illness might terminate in death.

It may here be noticed that, in the summer of 1694, Locke became one of the original proprietors of the Bank of England, which, having been projected by a merchant named William Paterson, had been established by Act of Parliament in April of that year, and invested with certain trading privileges, on condition that it should lend its capital to the Government at eight per cent. interest. The plan had encountered great opposition, especially among the landed gentry, and had only been carried through the strenuous exertions of Montague and the Whig party. Locke subscribed 500*l.*, a considerable sum in those days.

CHAPTER VI.

NOTWITHSTANDING his retirement to Oates, and his incessant literary activity, Locke never lost his interest in
politics, and, as the friend and admirer of men like Monmouth, Somers, and Clarke, he must always have exercised
a considerable influence on the policy of the whig party.
In the spring of 1695 he seems to have taken a primary
share in determining a measure which, for a time, divided
the Houses of Lords and Commons, and which must have
enlisted his warmest sympathies. This was the repeal of
the Licensing Act. The English Press had never been
wholly free, and the Act of Charles II., which was still
in force, was peculiarly stringent. Occasion had been
taken by the Commons, when it was proposed, in the
session of 1694-5, to renew certain temporary statutes, to
strike out this particular statute from the list. The Lords
dissented, and re-inserted it. The Commons refused to
accept the amendment. A conference of both Houses
took place, Clarke of Chipley being the leading manager
on the part of the Commons, and the result was that the
Lords waived their objections. The paper of reasons
tendered by the Commons' managers on this occasion is
said, by a writer in the *Craftsman* for November 20th,

1731, to have been drawn up by Locke. As Clarke was one of his most intimate friends, and as the Reasons correspond pretty closely with a paper of criticisms on the Act written by Locke, this statement is probably true, so far at least as concerns their substance. The arguments employed are mainly practical, consisting of objections in detail, and pointing out inconveniences, financial and otherwise, which resulted from the operation of the Act. But these arguments, " suited to the capacity of the parliamentary majority," did, as Macaulay has remarked, what Milton's *Areopagitica* had failed to do, and a vote, " of which the history can be but imperfectly traced in the Journals of the House, has done more for liberty and for civilization than the Great Charter or the Bill of Rights." Locke's paper of criticisms, which is published *in extenso* in *Lord King's Life,* asks very pertinently, " why a man should not have liberty to print whatever he would speak, and be answerable for the one, just as he is for the other, if he transgresses the law in either." He then offers a suggestion, to take the place of the licensing provisions :—" Let the printer or bookseller be answerable for whatever is against law in the book, as if he were the author, unless he can produce the person he had it from, which is all the restraint ought to be upon printing." It appears from this paper that the monopoly of the Stationers' Company had become so oppressive that books printed in London could be bought cheaper at Amsterdam than in St. Paul's Church Yard. Except for the few monopolists, the book-trade had been ruined in England. But then, he reflects, " our ecclesiastical laws seldom favour trade, and he that reads this Act with attention will find it upse" (that is, highly) " ecclesiastical."

This question had hardly been settled before Locke had

another opportunity of influencing legislation on a subject which absorbed much of his interest, and on which he had already employed his pen. Probably at no time in the history of our country has the condition of the coinage become so burning a question, or caused such wide-spread distress, as in the years immediately succeeding the Revolution. To understand the monetary difficulties occasioned by clipping the coin, it must be remembered that, at the time of which I am speaking, two kinds of silver money (if we neglect the imperfectly milled money which was executed between 1561 and 1663) were in circulation, hammered money with unmarked rims, and what was called milled money, from being made in a coining-mill, with a legend on the rim of the larger and graining on the rim of the smaller pieces. The latter kind of coins, too, had the additional advantage of being almost perfectly circular, while the shape of the former was almost always more or less irregular. The hammered money, it is plain, could be easily clipped or pared, whereas the milling was an absolute protection against this mode of fraud. Though milling, in much its present form, had been introduced into our mint in the year 1663, and then became the exclusive mode of coining, the old hammered money still continued to be legal tender ; and, as the milled money was always worth its weight in silver, and the hammered money was generally current at something much above its intrinsic worth, the milled money was naturally melted down or exported abroad, leaving the hammered money in almost exclusive possession of the field. The milled money disappeared almost as fast as it was coined, and the hammered money was clipped and pared more and more, till it was often not worth half or even a third of the sum for which it passed. At Oxford, indeed, a hundred pounds' worth

of the current silver money, which ought to have weighed
four hundred ounces, was found to weigh only a hundred
and sixteen.   Every month the state of things was becoming worse and worse.   The cost of commodities was
constantly rising, and every payment of any amount involved endless altercations.   In a bargain not only had
the price of the article to be settled, but also the value of
the money in which it was to be paid.   A guinea, which
at one place counted for only twenty-two shillings, would
at another fetch thirty, and might have brought far more,
had not the Government fixed that sum as the maximum
at which it would be taken in the payment of taxes.   Thus,
all commercial transactions had become disarranged, no
one knew what he was really worth, or what any commo-
dity might cost him a few months hence.   Macaulay,
who has given a most graphic description of the financial
condition of the country at this time, hardly exaggerates
when he says, "It may be doubted whether all the
misery which had been inflicted on the English nation in
a quarter of a century by bad kings, bad ministers, bad
parliaments, and bad judges, was equal to the misery
caused in a single year by bad crowns and bad shillings."
Almost from the moment of his return to England, Locke
had felt the-gravest anxiety on this subject.   "When at
my lodgings in London," says Lady Masham, speaking of
the time immediately succeeding the revolution, "the
company there, finding him often afflicted about a matter
which nobody else took any notice of, have rallied him
upon this uneasiness as being a visionary trouble, he has
more than once replied, 'We might laugh at it, but it
would not be long before we should want money to send
our servants to market with for bread and meat,' which
was so true, five or six years after, that there was not a

family in England who did not find this a difficulty."
The letter on " Some Considerations of the Consequences
of Lowering of Interest and Raising the Value of Money,"
the latter part of which dealt with this question, is dated
as early as November 7, 1691, and had been, in the main,
as he tells us, put into writing about twelve months before.
Here he not only points out the intolerable character of
the grievances under which the nation was labouring, but
also protests most emphatically against one of the proposed
methods of remedying them, namely, "raising the value
of money," as it was called ; that is, depreciating the
intrinsic value of the money coined, or raising the denomination, so, for instance, as to put into a crown-piece or
a shilling, when coined, less than the customary amount
of silver.   To the consideration of this scheme, which at
one time found much favour, we shall soon see that he had
occasion to recur.   Universal as were the complaints about
the existing state of things, no active measures, if we except
wholesale and frequent hangings for "clipping the coin,"
and increased measures of vigilance for the purpose of
detecting the delinquents, were taken for stopping the evil,
until the year 1695.   Under the malign ascendancy of
Danby, the Government had other views and objects than
to ameliorate the condition of the people.   But, in the
years 1694 and 1695, other and more enlightened statesmen were gradually winning their way into the royal
councils, or beginning to occupy a more important position
in them.   For at this period, we must recollect, the high
officers of state were not all, as now, necessarily of one uni-
form political pattern.   In April, 1694, immediately after the
establishment of the Bank of England, Charles Montague,
afterwards Lord Halifax, one of the greatest of English
financiers, had been made Chancellor of the Exchequer.

And, on occasion of the king's departure for the Continent in May, 1695, two of Locke's most intimate friends, Lord Keeper Somers and the Earl of Pembroke, were nominated among the seven Lords Justices, who were to govern the kingdom during William's absence. To discerning and judicious statesmen like Somers and Montague it must have been quite apparent that the penal laws for protecting the coinage were altogether inadequate to the purpose. The gains to be made were so large and so easily obtained, that men were ready to run the risk of the punishment. And, moreover, even if the crime were detected, the punishment was by no means certain or unattended with sympathy. Great as were the suffering and inconveniences inflicted on the people by these practices, the punishment of death appeared to many to be in excess of the offence. Juries were often unwilling to convict, and the disgrace incurred by the criminal was very different from that which attended the murderer or the ordinary thief. That wise financial legislation, and not the more stringent execution of the penal laws, was the true and only effectual mode of eradicating the disease, was at length recognized by the Government, and the new Lords Justices soon set about to devise the remedy. To Locke, who was well known to have been the author of the pamphlet which appeared on the subject in 1692, they naturally turned for advice. In the early part of October, while the king was on his way back from his successful campaign in the Netherlands, he was summoned up from Oates to confer with them. Writing to Molyneux the next month, and informing him of the fact, he adds with characteristic modesty : " This is too publicly known here to make the mentioning of it to you appear vanity in me." Notwithstanding the subordinate part which Locke here seems to

assign to himself, there can be no doubt that his share in
the measures of the Government, as ultimately matured,
was a principal, if not the principal, one.   That legislative
measures would now be taken, there was no longer any
question.   But the danger of which Locke was chiefly
afraid, was the raising the denomination of the coin, or,
in other words, the legalized depreciation of the currency,
a scheme against which he had formerly protested, and
which was now officially recommended to the Government
by one of their own subordinates, William Lowndes.
Orders had been given to Lowndes, who, after many
years of good service in a subordinate capacity, had
recently been appointed Secretary to the Treasury, to
collect statistics relating to the monetary condition of the
country, and to report on the most practicable methods of
re-coining the current silver money.   In executing the former part of his task, he left no doubt as to the necessity
of speedily applying some remedy.   The silver coins
brought into the exchequer during three months of 1695
ought to have weighed 221,418 ounces.   Their actual
weight was 113,771 ounces, or barely over one-half. In consequence of the vitiating, diminishing, and counterfeiting
of the current moneys, he says, " it is come to pass
that great contentions do daily arise amongst the king's
subjects in fairs, markets, shops, and other places
throughout the kingdom, about the passing and refusing
of the same, to the great disturbance of the public peace.
Many bargains, doings, and dealings are totally prevented
and laid aside, which lessens trade in general." The
necessity of setting the price of commodities according to
the value of the money to be received, is, he considers,
" one great cause of raising the price, not only of merchan-
dise, but even of edibles and other necessaries for the

sustenance of the common people, to their great grievance."
So far, his political economy was perfectly sound, but, when
he comes to discuss the question of re-coinage, he advocates,
without any misgiving, a scheme for the depreciation of the currency to the extent of one-fifth. A crown-
piece was henceforth to count as 6s. 3d., and the nominal
value of half-crowns, shillings, and sixpences was to be
raised proportionately. Locke, with his clearer mind, saw,
of course, that this would only be for the state to do
systematically and by law the very same thing for which
the clippers were being hanged. It would be to legalize
the disarrangement of all monetary transactions, and to
deprive every creditor of one-fifth of his debts. Montague
and Somers were as clear on this point as he was, and
Somers at once urged him to reply. Locke had returned to
Oates, in consequence of the sudden death of Mrs. Cudworth, on the 16th of November, and at once set about
his answer.

This tract, which formed a pamphlet of more than
a hundred pages, was submitted to the Lords Justices,
printed, and published before the end of December. It
was entitled, *Further Considerations concerning Raising
the Value of Money*, and simplified and enforced the
arguments contained in a previous pamphlet which Locke
had also drawn up for the use of the Lords Justices earlier
in the year, under the title, *Some Observations on a Printed
Paper, entitled, For Encouraging the Coining Silver
money in England, and after for keeping it here*.
Meanwhile, Montague had, under the sanction of a com-
mittee of the whole House, introduced his resolutions into
the House of Commons, and there can be little doubt
that, in drawing up these, he and the Lords Justices
had been assisted by Locke. Any way, the resolutions

embodied in the main the opinions which Locke had been
so instrumental in impressing on those in authority.   The
old standard value of the silver pieces was to be retained
both as to weight and fineness, the point for which he
had fought so persistently.   The clipped pieces were, after
a certain day, only to be received in payment of taxes, or
in loans to the exchequer; after a further day, they were
to cease to be legal tender altogether.   All the hammered
money, as it came into the mint in payment of loans or
taxes, was to be re-coined as milled money, and the loss to
be borne by the Exchequer.   When the resolution that the
old standard was to be retained was put to the House, it
was challenged, and an amendment moved by those who
were of Lowndes' opinion, that the word "both" be
omitted.   On a division, there were 225 for retaining the
word, and 114 against.   The House, thus, by a large
majority, affirmed what all economists would now regard
as an elementary principle of finance.   A Bill embodying
the resolution was soon passed, but, in consequence of
difficulties with the Lords, had to be dropped.   A fresh
Bill was introduced on the 13th of January, substantially
embodying the same provisions as the old Bill, and was
hurried through its various stages so fast, that it received
the Royal Assent on the 21st of January, 1695-6.   Up
to the 4th of May, 1696, the clipped money was to be
received in payment of taxes, and up to the 24th of June,
for loans or other payments into the Exchequer.   But
after the 10th of February ensuing, it was to cease to be
legal tender in ordinary payments.   Thus, in spite of much
temporary inconvenience caused by the scarcity of money
during the time of transition, the silver coinage of the
country was, once for all, put upon a sound basis.   Late
as Locke's pamphlet appeared, it probably helped to

facilitate the passage of the Bill through the two Houses,
as the reiterated statement of his opinions had undoubtedly
contributed in very large measure to shape and confirm
the action of the government.   It may be mentioned that
the loss to the Exchequer, estimated as 1,200,000*l.*, was
made up by the imposition of a house tax and window tax,
the former of which still continues, while the latter
existed within the memory of many men now only of
middle age.

Great as is the debt which philosophy owes to Locke's
Essay, constitutional theory to his treatises on government, the freedom of religious speculation to his Letters
on Toleration, and the ways of " sweet reasonableness " to
all these, and indeed to all his works, it would form a
nice subject of discussion whether mankind at large has
not been more benefited by the share which he took in
practical reforms than by his literary productions.   It
would undoubtedly be too much to affirm that, without
his initiative or assistance, the state of the coinage would
never have been reformed, the monopoly of the Stationers'
Company abolished, or the shackles of the Licensing Act
struck off.   But had it not been for his clearness of
vision, and the persistence of his philanthropic efforts,
these measures might have been indefinitely retarded or
clogged with provisos and compromises which might have
robbed them of more than half their effects.   A generation
ago it was the fashion in many circles to speak con-
temptuously of the writers and statesmen of William's
reign, and even now but scant and grudging justice is
often done to them.   The admirers of mystical philosophy
and romantic politics may, however, fairly be challenged
to show that their heroes, whether in letters or action,
have borne equal fruit with the vigorous understanding

and plain, direct, practical common-sense of men like
Halifax, Somers, and Locke.

It has already been stated that soon after his return to
England Locke was appointed a Commissioner of Appeals,
a post which, though not entirely without duties, seems
to have taken up but little of his time.   One of his letters
to Clarke shows the difficulty of forming a quorum, and
perhaps illustrates the fact that when the duties of an
office are slight, they are generally neglected altogether.
But towards the end of the year 1695 the government,
now virtually under the leadership of Somers, determined
to revive the council of trade and plantations of which,
it will be recollected, Locke had been Secretary when
Shaftesbury's counsels were in the ascendant at the court
of Charles II., as far back as the year 1673.   At first
there were some difficulties with the king, but ultimately,
on the 15th of May, 1696, he was induced to issue the
patent appointing and defining the duties of a commission.
Besides the great officers of state, there were to be certain
paid commissioners, with a salary of 1000l. a year, of
whom Locke was one.   His name was inserted in the first
draft of the commission without his express consent, and
he appears, as we can well understand, to have accepted
the office only with extreme reluctance.   Writing to
Molyneux, who had congratulated him on the appointment, he says with evident sincerity :—

" Your congratulation I take as you meant, kindly and seriously, and, it may be, it is what another would rejoice in; but
'tis a preferment I shall get nothing by, and I know not whether
my country will, though that I shall aim at with all my endeavours.   Riches may be instrumental to so many good purposes
that it is, I think, vanity rather than religion or philosophy to

pretend to contemn them. But yet they may be purchased too dear. My age and health demand a retreat from bustle and business, and the pursuit of some inquiries I have in my thoughts makes it more desirable than any of those rewards which public employments tempt people with. I think the little I have enough, and do not desire to live higher or die richer than I am. And therefore you have reason rather to pity the folly, than congratulate the fortune, that engages me in the whirlpool."

The duties of the commission could hardly have been more widely defined than they were. It was to be at once a Board of Trade, a Poor-Law Board, and a Colonial Office. The commissioners were to inquire into the general condition of trade in the country, both internal and external, and " to consider by what means the several useful and profitable manufactures already settled in the kingdom may be further improved ; and how, and in what manner, new and profitable manufactures may be introduced." They were also " to consider of some proper methods for setting on work and employing the poor of the kingdom, and making them useful to the public, and thereby easing our subjects of that burthen." Finally, they were to inform themselves of the present condition of the plantations, as the colonies were then called, not only in relation to commerce, but also to the administration of government and justice, as well as to suggest means of rendering them more useful to the mother country, especially in the supply of naval stores. Here, surely, was work enough for men far younger and more vigorous than Locke, but, having undertaken the duties of the office, he appears in no way to have spared himself. In the summer and autumn months he resided in London, and attended the meetings of the board personally, often day after day, and in the evening as well as the day-time.

In the winter and spring his health compelled him to reside at Oates, but he was constantly sending up long minutes for the use of his colleagues. Mr. Fox Bourne, who has been carefully through the proceedings of the commission, informs us that Locke was altogether its presiding genius. He was a member of this board a little over four years, having been compelled by increasing ill-health, or, as the minutes of the council put it, "finding his health móre and more impaired by the air of this city," to resign on the 28th of June, 1700. The king, we are told by Lady Masham, was most unwilling to receive his resignation, "telling him that, were his attendance ever so small, he was sensible his continuance in the commission would be useful to him, and that he did not desire he should be one day in town on that account to the prejudice of his health." Locke, however, was too conscientious to retain a place with large emoluments, of which he felt that he could no longer perform the duties to his own satisfaction. It is interesting to find that his successor was Matthew Prior, the poet.

When we have seen the wide powers of the commission, we hardly need feel surprise that its business was multifarious. It at once set to work to collect evidence of the state of trade in the colonies, of our commercial relations with foreign ports, of the condition of the linen and paper manufactures at home, of the number of paupers in the kingdom, and the mode of their relief, as well as to devise means for increasing the woollen trade and preventing the exportation of wool. Locke was specially commissioned " to draw up a scheme of some method of determining differences between merchants by referees that might be decisive without appeal." In the winter of 1696-7, finding that his work followed him to Oates, and being then

apparently in a feebler state of health than usual, he made
an ineffectual attempt to escape from his new employment,
but Somers refused to hand in his resignation to the king.
From a letter to Molyneux we find that it was not
simply his ill-health, but the "corruption of the age,"
which made him averse to continuing in office. And we
can well understand how troublesome, and apparently
hopeless, it must have been to deal with the various
threatened interests of that time, when monopolies,
patents, and pensions were regarded by the governing
classes almost as a matter of course.

In the summer of 1697 the principal subject which
engaged the attention of the commission was the best
means of discouraging the Irish woollen manufacture, and
of, at the same time, encouraging the Irish linen manufacture. Each commissioner was invited to bring up a
separate report. Three did so. Locke's was the one
selected, and, with slight alterations, was signed by the
other commissioners on the 31st of August, and forwarded
almost immediately afterwards to the Lords Justices.
This interesting state-document proceeds entirely upon
the notions of protection to native industries which were
then almost universally current among statesmen and
merchants. The problems were to secure to England the
monopoly of what was then regarded as its peculiar and
appropriate manufacture, the woollen trade, and to assign
to Ireland, in return for the restrictions imposed upon
her, some compensating branch of industry. According
to the ideas then commonly prevalent the scheme was
perfectly equitable to both countries. But, naturally,
the interests of England are put in the foreground. The
interests of the Irish people, however, were not to be
neglected, and what Locke doubtless conceived as full com-

pensation was to be given them for the loss of their woollen trade. " And since it generally proves ineffectual, and we conceive it hard to endeavour to drive men from the trade they are employed in by bare prohibition, without offering them at the same time some other trade which, if they please, may turn to account, we humbly propose that the linen manufacture be set on foot, and so encouraged in Ireland as may make it the general trade of that country as effectually as the woollen manufacture is, and must be, of England." Linen cloth and all other manufactures made of flax or hemp, without any mixture of wool, were to be exported to all places duty free, as indeed had already been provided by Act of Parliament with regard to England. One method by which Locke proposed to encourage the linen manufacture in Ireland runs so counter to modern notions with regard both to the education of the poor and to freedom of employment, that it may be interesting to the reader to see the suggestion at length :—

" And, because the poorest earning in the several parts of the linen manufacture is at present in the work of the spinners, who therefore need the greatest encouragement, and ought to be increased as much as possible, that therefore spinning schools be set up in such places and at such distances as the directors shall appoint, where whoever will come to learn to spin shall be taught gratis, and to which all persons that have not forty shillings a year estate shall be obliged to send all their children, both male and female, that they have at home with them, from six to fourteen years of age, and may have liberty to send those also between four and six if they please, to be employed there in spinning ten hours in the day when the days are so long, or as long as it is light when they are shorter; provided always that no child shall be obliged to go above two miles to any such school."

Then there follow many other minute and paternal

regulations of the same kind, the object of which was to
turn the whole Irish nation into spinners, and to supply
with linen not only " the whole kingdom of England," but
foreign markets as well.   The Irish authorities, however,
were meanwhile preparing a scheme of their own, and,
after controversies between the English and Irish officials,
extending over more than two years, Locke's plan was
finally laid aside in favour of that of Louis Crommelin.
Besides the attempt to monopolize the woollen trade for
England and the linen trade for Ireland, much of the time
of the Council was devoted to schemes for the protection
of native industries, by forbidding or throwing obstacles
in the way of importation and exportation.   But Locke
and his colleagues were here only following the track
marked out for them by the ordinary opinion of the time.

The main subject which occupied the attention of the
Council in the autumn of 1697 was the employment of the
idle or necessitous poor.   From the beginning of its
sessions, it had been collecting evidence on this subject,
and, in September of this year, it was decided that each
commissioner should draw up a scheme of reform, to be
submitted to the Council.   As had been the case with his
report on the Irish linen manufacture, Locke's was the one
selected.   From a variety of causes, however, his suggestions were never carried into effect, and the various efforts
of William's Government to deal with the gigantic
problem of pauperism proved abortive.

Locke's paper of suggestions assumes as a datum what
was always regarded at this time as an axiom of poor-law
legislation, namely, that it is the duty of each individual
parish to maintain and employ its own poor, having, as a
set-off, the right of coercing the able-bodied to work.
Pernicious and partial as this principle was, we should

H

have more occasion for surprise if we found Locke contravening it than conforming to it. The merit of his paper is that it offers excellent suggestions for minimizing the evils necessarily attaching to the system then in vogue. The recent growth of pauperism he refers to " relaxation of discipline and corruption of manners, virtue and industry being as constant companions on the one side as vice and idleness are on the other. The first step, therefore," he continues, " towards the setting of the poor on work ought to be a restraint of their debauchery by a strict execution of the laws provided against it, more particularly by the suppression of superfluous brandy-shops and unnecessary ale-houses, especially in country parishes not lying upon great roads." He then proposes a series of provisions, sufficiently stringent, for the purpose of compelling the idle and able-bodied poor to work, stating that, upon a very moderate computation, above one half of those who receive relief from the parishes are able to earn their own livelihood. In maritime counties, all those not physically or mentally incapacitated, who were found begging out of their own parish without a pass, were to be compelled to serve on board one of his Majesty's ships, under strict discipline, for three years. In the inland counties, all those so found begging were to be sent to the nearest house of correction for a like period. But, besides the able-bodied paupers, there were a great number not absolutely unable or unwilling to do something for their livelihood, and yet prevented by age or circumstances from wholly earning their own living. For these he proposes to find employment in the woollen or other manufactures, so as, at all events, to diminish the cost of their maintenance to the public, and at the same time increase the industrial resources of the country One of the most distinctive features of Locke's scheme was the proposal to set up working-schools for spinning or knitting, or some other industrial occupation, in each parish, " to which the children of all such as demand relief of the parish, above three and under fourteen years of age, whilst they live at home with their parents, and are not otherwise employed for their livelihood by the allowance of the overseers of the poor, shall be obliged to come." The children were to be fed at school, and this mode of relief was to take the place of the existing allowance in money paid to a father who had a large number of children, which, we are not surprised to learn, was frequently spent in the ale-house, whilst those for whose benefit it was given were left to perish for want of necessaries. The food of the children of the poor at that time, we are told, was seldom more than bread and water, and often there was a very scanty supply of that. Another advantage which Locke proposed to effect by the institution of these schools was the moral and religious instruction of the children. They would be obliged to come constantly to church every Sunday, along with their schoolmasters or dames, " whereby they would be brought into some sense of religion, whereas ordinarily now, in their idle and loose way of bringing up, they are as utter strangers both to religion and morality as they are to industry." One further provision of this scheme may be noticed, as offering some mitigation of the parochial system of relief which then obtained, namely, " that in all cities and towns corporate the poor's tax be not levied by distinct parishes, but by one equal tax throughout the whole corporation."

The anxiety of the king to retain Locke on the Commission has already been mentioned. It would appear that they were in not infrequent conference, and we know

that the king entertained a very high opinion both of his
integrity and of his political capacity. A good deal of
mystery attaches to one of their interviews, but the explanation of it proffered by Mr. Fox Bourne possesses, at
any rate, considerable plausibility. One bitter January
morning, in the winter of 1697-8, while Locke was at
Oates, he received a pressing summons from the king to
repair to Kensington. He was at the time suffering more
than ordinarily from the bronchial affection to which he
was constantly subject, and Lady Masham attempted to
dissuade him from running the risk of the journey, but in
vain. When he returned, the only account that he would
give of the interview was that " the king had a desire to
talk with him about his own health, as believing that
there was much similitude in their cases." It appears,
however, from a letter addressed by Locke to Somers a
few days after his return to Oates, that the king had
offered him some important employment, and that he had
excused himself on the ground of his weak health, and his
inexperience in that kind of business, the business being
such as required "skill in dealing with men in their
various humours, and drawing out their secrets." Mr.
Fox Bourne forms the reasonable conjecture that Locke
had been asked to go as right-hand man to William Ben-
tinck, Earl of Portland, who had just been nominated as
special ambassador to the Court of France. The peace of
Ryswick had been ratified in the previous November, and
the mission to Louis XIV. was, of course, one requiring
great tact and sagacity. William had strongly urged Locke,
some years before, to represent him on another very important mission, the one to the Elector of Brandenburg,
and it may be that, on the present occasion, no fitter
person occurred to him. Any way, the employment was

one which would have advanced Locke in riches and honour; but as such, glad as he might have been to serve his country disinterestedly to the best of his power, it had no attractions for him. "He must have a heart strongly touched with wealth or honours who, at my age, and labouring for breath, can find any great relish for either of them."

On one occasion Locke accompanied the king, the latter going *incognito*, to a meeting of the Society of Friends, where they listened to the famous Quaker preacheress, Rebecca Collier. Locke afterwards sent her a parcel of sweetmeats, with a very complimentary letter, and is said to have found the meeting so agreeable that it removed his objections to a female ministry.

With his resignation of the Commissionership of the Board of Trade, in the summer of 1700, Locke's public life comes to an end. His friend Somers had been sacrificed to the incessant and malignant attacks of the Tories, and dismissed from the Chancellorship, in the previous spring, and to those statesmen who were inspired by a sincere and simple desire for the well-being of their country, the political outlook had become anything but cheerful. The condition of Locke's health was quite a sufficient reason for his desiring to be relieved of the anxieties of office; but we can hardly doubt that, on other grounds as well, he was glad to escape from so intricate a maze as the field of politics bade fair soon to become.

CHAPTER VII.

In order to resume the thread of Locke's literary and
domestic life, it is now necessary to go back two or three
years. I have already spoken of no less than three literary
controversies in which he found himself engaged, one on
financial, and two on religious questions. Of the latter,
one was occasioned by the publication of the *Letter on
Toleration*, the other by that of the *Reasonableness of
Christianity*. The *Essay* also had been attacked by
Norris and other writers, including one very acute antago-
nist, John Serjeant, or Sergeant, a Roman Catholic priest,
but to these critics Locke did not see fit to reply. The
strictures on Norris only appear among his posthumous
works. But in the autumn of 1696 Stillingfleet, Bishop
of Worcester, in his *Discourse in Vindication of the
Doctrine of the Trinity*, pointedly drew attention to the
principles of the *Essay*, as favouring anti-Trinitarian
doctrine. Stillingfleet's position and reputation appeared
to demand an answer, and before the year, according to
the old style, was out, Locke's *Letter to the Bishop of
Worcester* was published. The Bishop's Answer, Locke's
Reply to the Answer, and the Bishop's "Answer to Mr.

Locke's Second Letter, wherein his notion of ideas is proved to be inconsistent with itself, and with the articles of the Christian faith," all followed, one on the other, within a few months.   The last letter of the series is " Mr. Locke's Reply to the Bishop of Worcester's Answer to his Second Letter," published in 1699.   Stillingfleet died soon after the publication of this pamphlet, and thus the voluminous controversy came to an end.   There can be no doubt that the antagonists were unequally matched. Stillingfleet was clumsy both in handling and argument, and constantly misrepresented or exaggerated the statements of his adversary.   On the other hand Locke, notwithstanding an unnecessary prolixity which wearies the modern reader, shows admirable skill and temper.   He deals tenderly with his victim, as if he loved him, but, none the less, never fails to despatch him with a mortal stab.   Stillingfleet, indeed, was no metaphysician, and not very much of a logician.   He did not see at all clearly where the orthodox doctrines were affected, and where they remained unaffected, by Locke's philosophy, and he no doubt considerably exaggerated the bearing of Locke's direct statements upon them.   At the same time, it is impossible to deny that his instincts were perfectly sound in apprehending grave dangers to the current theological opinions, and still more, perhaps, to the established mode of expressing them, from the " new way of ideas." Religious, and even devout, as are those portions of the *Essay* in which Locke has occasion expressly to mention the leading principles of the Christian faith, yet his handling of many of the metaphysical terms and notions which modern divines, whether Catholic or Protestant, had taken on trust from their predecessors, the fathers and schoolmen, was well calculated to alarm those who had

the interests of theological orthodoxy at heart. The playful freedom with which he discusses the idea of substance
seemed, not unreasonably, to strike at the terminology of
the Athanasian Creed, while, most unreasonably, his
resolution of personal identity into present and recollected
states of consciousness appeared inconsistent with the
doctrine of the Resurrection of the Dead. A far more
powerful solvent, however, of the unreflecting and com-
placent orthodoxy, into which established churches, and,
in fact, all prosperous religious communities, are apt to
lapse, was to be found in the general drift and tendency
rather than in the individual tenets of Locke's philosophy.
And this fact, though only very dimly and confusedly,
Stillingfleet appears to have seen. To insist that words
shall always stand for determinate ideas, to attempt to
trace ideas to their original sources, and to propose to discriminate between the certainty and varying probabilities of
our beliefs, according to the nature of the evidence on
which they rest, is to encourage a state of mind diametri-
cally the opposite of that which humbly and thankfully
accepts the words of the religious teacher, without doubt
and without inquiry. To the religious teacher whose own
beliefs rest on no previous inquiry, who has never
acquired " a reason for the faith that is in him," such a
state of mind must necessarily be not only inconvenient
but repulsive, and hence we have no right to feel surprised
when an attempt is made to expose it to popular odium,
or to fasten on those who entertain it injurious or oppro-
brious epithets. The old-standing feud, of which Plato
speaks, between poetry and philosophy, has in great
measure been transferred, in these latter times, to philosophy and theology. But, in both cases, the antagonism
is an unnecessary one. The highest art is compatible

with the most profound speculation. And so we may venture to hope that the simple love of truth, combined with the charity " which never faileth," will lead men not further away from the Divine presence, but nearer to, and into it.

Here I thankfully take leave of the mass of controversial literature, in the writing of which so much of Locke's latter life was spent. The controversies were not of his own seeking, and, from all that we know of his temper and character, must have been as distasteful to him as they are wearisome to us. But prolonged and reiterated controversy was of the habit of the time, and no man who cared candidly and unreservedly to express his opinions on any important question could hope to escape from it.

In the autumn of 1697, while the controversy with Stillingfleet was at its hottest, Locke wrote to Molyneux : —" I had much rather be at leisure to make some additions to my book of Education and my Essay on Human Understanding, than be employed to defend myself against the groundless, and, as others think, trifling quarrel of the bishop." He was at this time engaged on preparing the fourth edition of the *Essay* for the press. In addition to this task, or rather as part of it, he was also employing himself on writing the admirable little tract on the Conduct of the Understanding, the contents of which I shall notice in a subsequent chapter. This treatise, which was not published till after his death, was originally intended as an additional chapter to the *Essay*. Speaking of it in one of his letters to Molyneux, he says :—"I have written several pages on this subject ; but the matter, the farther I go, opens the more upon me, and I cannot yet get sight of any end of it. The title of the chapter will be 'Of the

Conduct of the Understanding,' which, if I shall pursue
as far as I imagine it will reach, and as it deserves, will, I
conclude, make the largest chapter of my Essay." It did
not, however, appear in the new edition, nor did Locke
ever reduce its parts into order, or put the finishing stroke
to it. He may, perhaps, have intended to revise it for a
subsequent edition of the *Essay*, but the fourth was the
last which appeared during his lifetime.

Before speaking of the literary labours which occupied
the last years of Locke's life, I may here conveniently
recur to his domestic history. Of his quiet life with the
Mashams little more need be said. Had Lady Masham
been his daughter, she could not have tended him more
carefully or lovingly, and had he been her father, he could
not have entertained a more sincere solicitude for the
welfare of her and her family. All Locke's friends were
welcome at Oates, and seem to have been regarded quite as
much as friends of the Mashams as of his own. And Oates
appears in every respect to have been as much Locke's home
as that of its owners. In the whole of his correspondence,
there does not appear the slightest trace of those petty
piques and annoyances, those small *désagréments*, which
are so apt to grow up among people who live much together, even when, at bottom, they entertain a deep love and
admiration for each other. On the side of the Mashams
we know that the tide of affection ran equally smooth.
Lady Masham and Esther acted as his nurses, and with one
or other of them he seems to have shared all his pursuits.
The intimacy and sweetness of these relations surely imply
as rare an amount of amiability of temper and power of
winning regard on the one side as of patience and devotion
on the other. But then Locke possessed the inestimable

gift of cheerfulness, which renders even the invalid's chamber a joy to those who enter it. All the glimpses we obtain of the life at Oates represent it as a gay and pleasant one, none the less gay and pleasant because its enjoyments were modest and rational. After complaining to Molyneux of the persistent asthma which confined him a close prisoner to the house during the winter of 1697-8, he adds, "I wish nevertheless that you were here with me to see how well I am; for you would find that, sitting by the fireside, I could bear my part in discoursing, laughing, and being merry with you, as well as ever I could in my life. If you were here (and, if wishes of more than one could bring you, you would be here to-day) you would find three or four in the parlour after dinner, who, you would say, passed their afternoons as agreeably and as jocundly as any people you have this good while met with." Locke's conversation is reported to have been peculiarly fascinating. He had a large stock of stories, and is said to have had a singularly easy and humorous way of telling them.

Among the more frequent guests at Oates at this time were Edward Clarke and his daughter Betty, Locke's "little wife," now fast growing up to womanhood, a son of Limborch, and a son of Benjamin Furly, both engaged in mercantile pursuits in London, and a young kinsman of Locke's own, Peter King, of whom I shall have more to say presently. One of the most anxiously expected guests, whose visits had been often promised and often deferred, was the correspondent of whom we have heard so much, William Molyneux. At length, after the rising of the British Parliament in the summer of 1698, the two friends met. Even on this occasion, Molyneux had been obliged to defer his promised visit for some weeks, on account of a recent trouble which he had brought on himself by the publication of a "home-rule" pamphlet, protesting against the interference of the English Parliament in Irish affairs. Both Houses had joined in an address to the king, praying for punishment on the offender, but the king, possibly through Locke's intervention, had wisely taken no notice of the petition. Any way, after the prorogation, Molyneux seems to have felt sufficiently secure to venture on a journey across the channel. He and Locke were together for some time both in London and at Oates. The friends, though they had been in such constant and intimate correspondence for six years, had never met before. We may easily imagine how warm was their greeting, how much they had to talk about, and how loath they were to separate. "I will venture to assert to you," wrote Molyneux on his return to Dublin, "that I cannot recollect, through the whole course of my life, such signal instances of real friendship, as when I had the happiness of your company for five weeks together in London. That part thereof especially which I passed at Oates has made such an agreeable impression on my mind that nothing can be more pleasing." Shortly after writing this letter, Molyneux died at the early age of forty-two. "His worth and his friendship to me," writes Locke in a letter to Burridge, the Latin translator of the *Essay*, "made him an inestimable treasure, which I must regret the loss of the little remainder of my life, without any hopes of repairing it any way." He then characteristically goes on to ask if there is any service he can render to Molyneux's son. "They who have the care of him cannot do me a greater pleasure than to give me the opportunity to show that my friendship died not with his father." One of the most amiable and attractive traits in Locke's character is the

eagerness which he always displayed in advising, encouraging, or helping forward the sons of his friends.
Any opportunity of doing so always gave him the most
evident satisfaction, as, from his correspondence, we see in
the case of Frank Masham, the two young Furlys, young
Limborch, and numerous others.

I must now no longer delay the introduction to the
reader of Locke's young cousin, Peter King.   Locke had
an uncle, Peter Locke, whose daughter Anne had married
Jeremy King, a grocer and salter in a substantial way of
business at Exeter.   Such a marriage was not necessarily
any disparagement to Anne Locke's family, as the present
line of demarcation between professional men and the
smaller gentry, on the one side, and substantial retail
tradesmen, on the other, hardly existed at that time.   They
had a son, Peter, born in 1669, who was consequently
Locke's first cousin once removed.   The boy seems for
some time to have been employed in his father's business,
but he had a voracious appetite for books, and showed a
decided talent for the acquisition of learning.   Locke, on
one of his visits to Exeter, discovered these qualities, and
persuaded Peter King's parents to allow him to change his
mode of life, and study for one of the learned professions.
Whether he went to any English school does not appear;
but, during Locke's stay in Holland, he resided for some
time in the University of Leyden.   His studies there
embraced at least classics, theology, and law; and when he
returned to England, apparently in 1690, he brought back
with him a pamphlet entitled, *An Enquiry into the Constitution and Discipline of the Primitive Church.*   As in
this treatise he maintained that Presbyterianism was the
original form of Church government, he probably never
had any serious intention, notwithstanding his theological

proclivities, of entering holy orders in the Established
Church.   Any way, in October, 1694, he was entered a
student of the Middle Temple, and in Trinity Term, 1698,
he was called to the Bar.   During his residence in London
as a law student, he must have been frequently at Oates,
and Locke must have frequently visited him in his
chambers in the Temple.   The first extant letter from
Locke to King, dated June 27th, 1698, at any rate
assumes intimacy and frequency of intercourse.   " Your
company here had been ten times welcomer than any the
best excuse you could send ; but you may now pretend to
be a man of business, and there can be nothing said to
you."   Very sound was the advice with which the elder
relative concluded his letter to the young barrister :
" When you first open your mouth at the bar, it should
be in some easy plain matter that you are perfectly master
of."   King's success in his profession was very rapid, and
he soon became one of the most popular counsel on the
Western Circuit.   In the general election of 1700 he
attained one of the first objects of ambition at which a
rising young barrister generally aims—a seat in the House
of Commons.   Owing, probably, to his cousin's influence
with the Whig leaders, he was returned for the small
borough of Beer Alston, in Devonshire, which he continued to represent in several successive Parliaments.
Locke, writing to him shortly before the meeting of Parliament, entreats him not to go circuit, as he had intended
to do, but to devote himself at once to his Parliamentary
duties.   " I am sure there was never so critical a time,
when every honest member of Parliament ought to watch
his trust, and that you will see before the end of the next
vacation."   The loss to his pocket, his good relative in-
timates, delicately enough, shall be amply made up to

him. King took his cousin's advice on this point, but, fortunately and wisely, did not take it on another. "My advice to you is not to speak at all in the house for some time, whatever fair opportunity you may seem to have." King was advised to communicate his "light or apprehensions" to some "honest speaker," who might make use of them for him. Locke, we must remember, was now becoming old, and though not, like many old men, jealous of his juniors, he could not escape the infirmity of all old men, that of exaggerating the youthfulness of youth, and so of insisting too stringently on the modesty becoming those in whom he was interested. King broke the ice soon after the meeting of Parliament, and Locke had the prudence and good-nature to show no resentment at his advice having been neglected. His cousin, however, never became a great Parliamentary speaker; but he soon gained a reputation for being a thoroughly sound lawyer and a thoroughly honest man. He rose successively to be Recorder of London, Lord Chief Justice of the Common Pleas, and Lord High Chancellor of England. He was also ennobled as Lord King of Ockham, and, by a very curious coincidence, his four sons in succession bore the same title. To one of his descendants, his great-grandson, also named Peter, we owe the publication of many documents and letters connected with Locke, and the biography so well known as *Lord King's Life of Locke*. The present representative of the family, and the direct descendant in the male line of Peter King, is the Earl of Lovelace. As Peter King was, to all intents, Locke's adopted son, we may thus regard Locke as the founder of an illustrious line in the English peerage, and there are certainly few, if any, of our ennobled families who can point to a founder whose name is so likely to be the heritage of all future ages.

King kept Locke well posted in all that went on in parliament, and seems also have been a constant visitor at Oates. Soon after his election, Sir Francis Masham had considerately proposed to Locke that his cousin should " steal down sometimes with him on Saturday, and return on Monday." On one of these occasions, in the Easter holidays of 1701, King was accompanied by young Lord Ashley, now become the third Earl of Shaftesbury. Locke had then surmounted his winter troubles, and his old pupil pronounces him as well as he had ever known him.

Amongst Locke's correspondents in these years was the celebrated physician, Dr. Sloane, now Secretary of the Royal Society, afterwards created Sir Hans Sloane. In writing to him at the end of the century, evidently in answer to a request, Locke proposes a scheme for rectifying the calendar. Notwithstanding the reformation which had already taken place in many foreign countries, it will be recollected that the English year then began on the 25th of March, instead of the 1st of January, and that, by reckoning the year at exactly $365\frac{1}{4}$ days, or at 11 m. 14 sec. longer than its actual length, our time lagged ten days behind that of most other European countries, as well as the real solar time. The inconvenience, especially in transactions with foreign merchants, had become very great. The advent of the new century, inasmuch as the centenary year would be counted as a leap-year in England, but not in other countries where the new style or Gregorian calendar prevailed, would add an eleventh day to the amount of discrepancy, and hence the subject was now attracting more than ordinary attention. Locke's remedy was to omit the intercalar day in the year 1700, according to the rule of the Gregorian calendar, as also for the ten next leap-years following, " by which easy way," he says, " we should in forty-four years insensibly return to the new style." " This," he adds, " I call an easy way, because it would be without prejudice or disturbance to any one's civil rights, which, by lopping off ten or eleven days at once in any one year, might perhaps receive inconvenience, the only objection that ever I heard made against rectifying our account." He also suggested that the year should begin, as in most other European countries, on the 1st of January. No change, however, was made till, by an Act of Parliament passed in 1750-1, it was ordered that the year 1752 should begin on the 1st of January, and that the day succeeding the 2nd of September in that year should be reckoned as the 14th. Locke's other correspondence with Sloane shows the interest which he still took in medical matters, and how ready he always was to expend time and thought on attending to the ailments of his poor neighbours at Oates.

During the latter years of Locke's life his principal literary employment consisted in paraphrasing and writing commentaries on some of St. Paul's epistles. He thought that this portion of Scripture offered peculiar difficulties, and finding, as he says, that he did not understand it himself, he set to work, rather for his own sake, and perhaps also that of the household at Oates, than with any view of publication, to attempt to clear up its obscurities. The labour was a work of love, and to a man of Locke's devout disposition, with almost a child-like confidence in the guidance of Scripture, the occupation must have afforded a peculiar solace in the intervals of his disease, and as he felt that he was rapidly approaching the confines of that other world which had so long been familiar to his thoughts. Though he was induced to consent to

I

the publication of these commentaries, and though he
himself prepared an introduction to them, they did not
appear till after his death.   They were then issued by
instalments, coming out at intervals between 1705 and
1707 inclusively.

Locke's political interests, always keen, were specially
active in the winter of 1701-2.   England was just then
on the point of engaging in the war of the Spanish Succession.   In the previous September an alliance against
France and Spain had been concluded between the em-
peror and the two great maritime powers, England and
Holland.   Almost immediately after the conclusion of
this treaty, James the Second had died at St. Germain,
and not only had the French king allowed his son to be
proclaimed King of England but had himself received
him with royal honours at the court of Versailles.   The
patriotic and protestant feeling of the country was thoroughly roused, and the new parliament, which met on
the 30th of December, was prepared to take the most
energetic measures for the purpose of supporting the
national honour and the Protestant succession.   The king's
speech, on opening the parliament, excited an outburst of
enthusiasm throughout the nation.   He conjured the
members to disappoint the hopes of their enemies by their
unanimity.   As he was ready to show himself the common
father of his people, he exhorted them to cast out the
spirit of party and division, so that there might no longer
be any distinction but between those who were friends to
the Protestant religion and the present establishment, and
those who wished for a popish prince and a French
government.   The speech was printed in English, Dutch,
and French, framed, and hung up, as an article of furniture, in the houses of good Protestants, both at home and

abroad.   Locke, writing to Peter King four days after the
meeting of parliament, asks him to send a copy of the
king's speech, "printed by itself, and without paring off
the edges."   He suggests that, in addition to what the
two Houses had done, the city of London and counties of
England should, "with joined hearts and hands return
his Majesty addresses of thanks for his taking such care
of them."   "Think of this with yourself," he says, "and
think of it with others who can and ought to think how
to save us out of the hands of France, into which we must
fall, unless the whole nation exert its utmost vigour, and
that speedily."   He is specially urgent on his cousin not
to leave town, or to think of circuit business, till the kingdom has been put in an effectual state of defence.   "I
think it no good husbandry for a man to get a few fees on
circuit and lose Westminster Hall."   By losing Westminster Hall he does not, apparently, mean losing the chance
of a judgeship, but forfeiting those rights and liberties,
and that personal and national independence which the
Revolution had only so lately restored.   "For, I assure
you, Westminster Hall is at stake, and I wonder how any
one of the house can sleep till he sees England in a better
state of defence, and how he can talk of anything else till
that is done."   But a majority, at least, of the House of
Commons was fully alive to its responsibilities ; enormous
supplies were voted, and almost every conceivable measure
was taken for securing the Protestant succession to the
crown.   A few days after Locke wrote the letter last
quoted, King William died.   His reflections on that event
or on the political prospects under William's successor,
we do not possess.

As the war proceeded, Locke's old friend, the Earl of
Monmouth, now become Earl of Peterborough, was en-

trusted with a naval expedition against the Spanish pos-
sessions in the West Indies.   He had a great desire to see
Locke before his departure, and, Locke being unable to
come up to London, he and the Countess drove down to
Oates about the middle of November, 1702.   It is
characteristic of the times that Locke was "much in
pain" about their getting back safely to town, the days being
then so short.   His young friend, Arent Furly, who was also
a protégé and frequent correspondent of Lord Shaftesbury,
went out as Lord Peterborough's secretary, and seems to
have acquitted himself in the position with marked
diligence and success.   The early promise which he gave,
however, was soon blighted.   This young play-fellow and
foster-child, as he might almost have been called, of Locke,
died only a few years after him, in 1711 or 1712.   Before
accompanying Lord Peterborough on his expedition, he
had been living for some time, first at Oates, and afterwards in lodgings in the neighbourhood, for the purpose of
learning English.

It is gratifying to find that, during the autumn of this
year, Locke had received a visit from Newton.   During
the discussion of the re-coinage question, and the active
operations which followed for the purpose of carrying out
the decisions of parliament, they must have been thrown
a good deal together.   Montague declared that, had it not
been for the energetic measures taken by Newton, as Warden of the Mint, the re-coinage would never have been
effected.   When, however, Newton came down to visit
Locke at Oates, in 1702, their conversation seems to have
turned mainly on theological topics.   Locke showed
Newton his notes upon the Corinthians, and Newton re-
quested the loan of them.   But, like most borrowers, he
neglected to return them, nor did he take any notice of

a letter from Locke, who was naturally very anxious
to recover his manuscript. Peter King was asked to try
to manage the matter. He was to call at Newton's residence in Jermyn Street, to deliver a second note, and to
find out, if he could, the reasons of Newton's silence,
and of his having kept the papers so long. But he
was to do this "with all the tenderness in the world,"
for "he is a nice man to deal with, and a little too
apt to raise in himself suspicions where there is no
ground." The emissary was also, if he could do it with
sufficient adroitness, to discover Newton's opinion of the
Commentary. But he was by no means to give the
slightest cause of offence. "Mr. Newton is really a very
valuable man, not only for his wonderful skill in mathematics, but in divinity too, and his great knowledge in the
scriptures, wherein I know few his equals. And therefore pray manage the whole matter so as not only to
preserve me in his good opinion, but to increase me in it ;
and be sure to press him to nothing but what he is forward in himself to do." In this letter Locke, notwithstanding the caution with which he felt it necessary to
approach one of so susceptible a temperament, says, " I
have several reasons to think him truly my friend." And
in this generous judgment there can be little doubt he
was right. The friends probably never met again, but
Newton is said to have paid a visit, on one of his journeys
perhaps from London to Cambridge, to Locke's tomb at
High Laver. Peter King succeeded in recovering the
manuscript, and at the same time or soon afterwards there
came a letter, criticizing one of Locke's interpretations,
but expressing a general opinion that the "paraphrase and
commentary on these two epistles is done with very great
care and judgment."

Something should here be said of two friends whom Locke had made in later life, one of whom seems to have been constantly about him during his last years. The less intimate of these was Samuel Bolde, a Dorsetshire clergyman, who had come forward, in 1697, to defend the *Reasonableness of Christianity* against Edwards' attacks, and who afterwards did Locke a similar service in replying to the assailants of the *Essay.* He was one of Locke's correspondents, and, once at least, paid him a visit at Oates. Bolde's outspokenness and independence of judgment naturally excited Locke's admiration. There are some memorable sentences in a letter written to him in 1699. " To be learned in the lump, by other men's thoughts, and to be in the right by saying after others, is the much easier and quieter way ; but how a rational man, that should inquire and know for himself, can content himself with a faith or a religion taken upon trust, or with such a servile submission of his understanding as to admit all and nothing else but what fashion makes passable among men, is to me astonishing. I do not wonder you should have, in many points, different apprehensions from what you meet with in authors. With a free mind, which unbiassedly pursues truth, it cannot be otherwise." After expanding these thoughts, and applying them to the study of Scripture, he goes on to advise Bolde how to supply a mental defect that he had complained of, namely, that "he lost many things because they slipped from him." The simple method was to write them down as they occurred. " The great help to the memory is writing," Bacon had said. Locke emphasizes the dictum, and adds, " If you have not tried it, you cannot imagine the difference there is in studying with and without a pen in your hand." " The thoughts that come unsought, and as it were dropped into the mind, are commonly the most valuable of any we have, and therefore should be secured, because they seldom return again."

The other friend, whose acquaintance had only been made during these later years, was Anthony Collins, who was not more than twenty-eight years of age when Locke died. Collins afterwards attained great celebrity as a Deistical writer, but none of his theological works appeared till some time after Locke's death. Locke, with his sincere and simple belief in the divine origin of the Christian Revelation, would doubtless, had he lived to see them, have been shocked with their matter, and still more with their style. But, at the present time, Collins presented him-self to him simply in the light of an ingenuous young man, with rare conversational powers and wide interests, and with what Locke valued far more, an eager desire to find out the truth. No one can have read the tracts, *An Inquiry concerning Human Liberty*, and *Liberty and Necessity*, without recognizing the acuteness and direct-ness of Collins' intellect, and these, we know, were quali-ties always peculiarly acceptable to Locke. Moreover, to encourage and bring forward younger men had invariably been one of his main delights. Hence we may, perhaps, abate our surprise at the apparently exaggerated language in which he addresses this friend, who was so much his junior in age, and who must have become known to him only so recently. "Why do you make yourself so neces-sary to me? I thought myself pretty loose from the world; but I feel you begin to fasten me to it again. For you make my life, since I have had your friendship, much more valuable to me than it was before." "If I were now setting out in the world, I should think it my great happiness to have such a companion as you, who had a relish for truth, would in earnest seek it with me, from whom I might receive it undisguised, and to whom I might communicate freely what I thought true. Believe it, my good friend, to love truth for truth's sake is the principal part of human perfection in this world and the seed-plot of all other virtues, and, if I mistake not, you have as much of it as I ever met with in anybody." Then he adds pathetically, but with a tone of hopefulness in the labours of others, which is not commonly found amongst old men, "When I consider how much of my life has been trifled away in beaten tracks, where I vamped on with others only to follow those that went before us, I cannot but think I have just as much reason to be proud as if I had travelled all England, and, if you will, France too, only to acquaint myself with the roads and be able to tell how the highways lie, wherein those of equipage, and even the herd too, travel. Now, methinks—and these are often old men's dreams—I see openings to truth and direct paths leading to it, wherein a little industry and application would settle one's mind with satisfaction, and leave no darkness or doubt. But this is at the end of my day, when my sun is setting ; and though the prospect it has given me be what I would not for anything be without—there is so much irresistible truth, beauty, and consistency in it—yet it is for one of your age, I think I ought to say for yourself, to set about it." What were those " openings to truth and direct paths leading to it "? Were they merely the delusive visions of an old man's fancies, or had he really formed wider conceptions of science, and pictured to himself more precise and fertile methods of reaching it ? The sciences, it is needless to observe, have grown vastly since Locke's day ; the methods of scientific research are far more numerous, more accurate, richer in their results. Had Locke, in his thoughts at this time, at all anticipated the courses which inquiry and knowledge have since taken ?

The letter to Collins, from which I have just quoted, was written on October 29, 1703. Within a year of that date, the end came. The wonder, indeed, is that, with his persistent malady, aggravated apparently in these latter years with other disorders, Locke's life had continued so long. The reasons are probably to be sought in his unfailing cheerfulness, in the variety of interests which diverted his mind from the thought of his own ailments, and in the judicious manner in which he regulated his exercise and diet. Of these personal traits, something may conveniently here be said. The remarkable cheerfulness of his disposition, his lively sense of humour, and his power of extracting amusement from all that was going on around him, have frequently come before us in the course of this biography. His temper was not moody, like that of so many men of letters, but pre-eminently sociable. When not actually engaged in his studies, he always liked to be in company, and enjoyed especially the society of young people and children. He had a happy knack of talking to his companions for the time being on the subjects which interested them most, and in this way he gained a very extensive knowledge of the various kinds of business and of a variety of arts and crafts. To working people he was often able to give very useful hints as to their own employments. This union of conversational qualities, grave and gay, invariably made him a welcome addition to any company, young or old, gentle or simple. An even temper, and a combination of happy gifts of this kind, will carry a man through much suffering, bodily and mental. From any mental troubles, on his own account,

Locke seems during these latter years of his life to have been remarkably free. From bodily suffering he was rarely exempt, but he always endured it with resignation, and endeavoured to obviate its causes by every precaution which his prudence or medical skill suggested. Thus, we have seen that, whenever it was possible, he preferred the quiet life and pure air of the country to the many attractions which the capital must have offered to a man with his wide acquaintance, and with so many political and literary interests. In diet he practised an abstemiousness very rare among men of that age. His ordinary drink was water, and to this habit he attributed not only his length of years, but also the extraordinary excellence of his eyesight. Till recently, a curious relic of Locke's water-drinking habits was preserved in the shape of a large mortar of spongy stone, which acted as a natural filter, and which he used to call his brew-house. He was assiduous in taking exercise, and was specially fond of walking and gardening. In the latter years of his life he used to ride out slowly every day after dinner. When advising his friend Clarke about his health, he says, " I know nothing so likely to produce quiet sleep as riding about gently in the air for many hours every day," and then, like a truly wise doctor, he adds, " If your mind can be brought to contribute a little its part to the laying aside troublesome ideas, I could hope this may do much." At last, when he was no longer able to sit on horseback, he commissioned Collins to have an open carriage specially made for him, the principle on which it was to be constructed being that " convenient carries it before ornamental."

In November, 1703, the Heads of Houses at Oxford— who at that time constituted the governing body, and through whose repressive and reactionary administration

the evil genius of Laud then and long afterwards continued to cast a blight on the University—resolved to
discourage the reading of Locke's *Essay*. The attempt
was futile, as they relied, not on coercion, but on the
influence of their authority, which appears to have been
held very cheap. Locke was now far too eminent a man
to be troubled by so anile a demonstration of folly. " I
take what has been done, as a recommendation of my
book to the world," he says, in a letter to Collins ; and then
he promises himself and his friend much merriment on the
subject when they next meet.

Locke's last literary labour appears to have been his
Fourth Letter for Toleration.   Jonas Proast, after a long
interval, had returned to the charge in a pamphlet published in 1704 ; and Locke, unfortunately, thought it
incumbent on him to reply, though he had long ceased to
pay any regard to the assailants of the *Essay*. The
Letter is unfinished. Its last words cannot have been
written long before Locke's death.

The winter of 1703-4 seems to have been peculiarly
trying to his health. He hardly expected to live through
it ; but he still maintained his cheerfulness, and followed
his usual employments. On the 11th of April, 1704, he
made his will—perhaps not his first. To most of his
friends, relatives, and dependents he left some remem-
brance ; but the bulk of his personal property he left to
Frank Masham and Peter King, the latter of whom was
sole executor and residuary legatee. All his manuscripts
were left to King. Many of these were published for the
first time by the seventh Lord King, in his *Life of Locke*.
His land he designedly did not will, and so it devolved
by law, in equal shares, on his two cousins, Peter King and
Peter Stratton.   His funeral was to be conducted without

any ostentation, and what it would otherwise have cost was to be divided amongst four poor labourers at Oates.

The approach of summer had not its usual restorative effect upon him. On the other hand, all the bad symptoms of his disease increased. To use his own expression, "the dissolution of the cottage was not far off." In a letter, written on the 1st of June, he earnestly pressed King to come to him, that he might pass some of the last hours of his life "in the conversation of one who is not only the nearest but the dearest to me of any man in the world." Both King and Collins seem to have visited him frequently during the last months of his life; and their society being cheerful, and the topics of their conversation interesting, he appears to have taken great pleasure in their company. He did not, however, find equal enjoyment in the visit of Dr. Edward Fowler, Bishop of Gloucester, who, like himself, was in a bad state of health. "I find two groaning people make but an uncomfortable concert." The moral he draws is, that men should enjoy their health and youth while they have it, "to all the advantages and improvements of an innocent and pleasant life," remembering that merciless old age is in pursuit of them. The lamp of life was now dimly flickering, but once more it burnt up in the socket before going out for ever. Peter King had been married on the 10th of September, and he and his bride must be received with all due honours at Oates. King was asked to cater for his own wedding feast, and goodly and dainty is the list of delicacies which he was to buy. But something, perhaps, might be omitted in which Mrs. King took special delight. "If there be anything that you can find your wife loves, be sure that provision be made of that, and plentifully, whether I have mentioned it or no."

The feast was to be cooked by "John Gray, who was bred up in my Lord Shaftesbury's kitchen, and was my Lady Dowager's cook." The wedded pair arrived at Oates towards the end of the month, and well can we picture to ourselves the pride and pleasure with which the genial old man entertained the wife of his cousin and adopted son—the adopted son whom he had rescued from the grocer's shop at Exeter, and whose future eminence he must now have pretty clearly foreseen. A few days after King left Oates, he solemnly committed to him by letter the care of Frank Masham. "It is my earnest request to you to take care of the youngest son of Sir Francis and Lady Masham in all his concerns, as if he were your brother. Take care to make him a good, an honest, and an upright man. I have left my directions with him to follow your advice, and I know he will do it; for he never refused to do what I told him was fit." Then, turning to King himself, he says, "I wish you all manner of prosperity in this world, and the everlasting happiness of the world to come. That I loved you, I think you are convinced."

Peter King certainly executed the dying request of his cousin, so far as Frank Masham's material interests were concerned. Soon after he became Lord Chancellor, Frank Masham was appointed to the newly constituted office of Accountant-General in the Court of Chancery, a lucrative post, conferring the same status as a Mastership.

Locke retained his faculties and his cheerfulness to the last; but he grew gradually weaker, day by day. "Few people," says Lady Masham, "do so sensibly see death approach them as he did." A few days before his death he received the sacrament from the parish minister, professing his perfect charity with all men, and his " sincere communion with the whole Church of Christ, by whatever name Christ's followers call themselves." In the last hours he talked much with the Mashams about their eternal concerns. As for himself, he had lived long enough, and enjoyed a happy life; but he looked forward to a better. At length, on the afternoon of the 28th of October, the spirit left him, and the earthly tabernacle was dissolved. His body is buried in the churchyard of High Laver, in a pleasant spot on the south side of the church. The Latin epitaph on the wall above the tomb was written by himself. It tells us that he had lived content with his own insignificance: that, brought up among letters, he had advanced just so far as to make an acceptable offering to truth alone: if the traveller wanted an example of good life, he would find one in the Gospel; if of vice, would that he could find one nowhere; if of mortality, there and everywhere.

" His death," says Lady Masham, " was, like his life, truly pious, yet natural, easy, and unaffected; nor can time, I think, ever produce a more eminent example of reason and religion than he was, living and dying.

CHAPTER VIII.

" WERE it fit to trouble thee," says Locke in his Epistle
to the Reader, " with the history of this *Essay*, I
should tell thee, that five or six friends meeting at my
chamber, and discoursing on a subject very remote from
this, found themselves quickly at a stand by the difficulties that rose on every side. After we had a while puzzled
ourselves, without coming any nearer a resolution of those
doubts which perplexed us, it came into my thoughts that
we took a wrong course; and that, before we set ourselves
upon inquiries of that nature, it was necessary to examine
our own abilities, and see what objects our understandings
were or were not fitted to deal with. This I proposed to
the company, who all readily assented; and thereupon it
was agreed that this should be our first inquiry."

This passage may serve not only to describe the occasion
of Locke's *Essay*, but also to indicate the circumstance
which constitutes the peculiar merit and originality of
Locke as a philosopher. The science which we now call
Psychology, or the study of mind, had hitherto, amongst
modern writers, been almost exclusively subordinated to
the interests of other branches of speculation. Some ex-
ception must, indeed, be made in favour of Hobbes and

Gassendi, Descartes and Spinoza, but all these authors
treated the questions of psychology somewhat cursorily,
while the two former seem usually to have had in view
the illustration of some favourite position in physics or
ethics, the two latter the ultimate establishment of some
proposition relating to the nature or attributes of God.
We may say then, without much exaggeration, that Locke
was the first of modern writers to attempt at once an independent and a complete treatment of the phenomena of
the human mind, of their mutual relations, of their causes
and limits.   His object was, as he himself phrases it, " to
inquire into the original, certainty, and extent of human
knowledge ; together with the grounds and degrees of
belief, opinion, and assent." This task he undertakes not
in the dogmatic spirit of his predecessors, but in the
critical spirit which he may be said to have almost in-
augurated.   As far as it is possible for a writer to divest
himself of prejudice, and to set to his work with a candid
and open mind, seeking help and information from all
quarters, Locke does so.   And the effect of his candour
on his first readers must have been enhanced by the fact,
not always favourable to his precision, that, as far as he
can, he throws aside the technical terminology of the
schools and employs the language current in the better
kinds of ordinary literature and the well-bred society of
his time.   The absence of pedantry and of *parti pris* in a
philosophical work was at that time so rare a recommendation that, no doubt, these characteristics contributed
largely to the rapid circulation and the general acceptance
of the *Essay*.

The central idea, which dominates Locke's work, is that
all our knowledge is derived from experience.   But this
does not strike us so much as a thesis to be maintained as

a conclusion arrived at after a vast amount of patient
thought and inquiry.   Have we any ideas independent of
experience ? or, as Locke phrases it, are there any Innate
Principles in the mind ?

"It is an established opinion amongst some men, that there
are in the Understanding, certain Innate Principles, some Primary Notions, κοιναὶ ἔννοιαι, characters, as it were, stamped
upon the mind of man, which the Soul receives in its very first
being and brings into the world with it."

This is the opinion which Locke examines and refutes
in the first, or introductory, book of the *Essay.*   It has
often been objected that he mistakes and exaggerates the
position which he is attacking.   And so far as his distinguished predecessor, Descartes, is concerned (though to
what extent Locke has him in mind, his habit of not
referring to other authors by name prevents us from
knowing), this is undoubtedly the case.   For Descartes,
though he frequently employs and accepts the expression
"innate notions" or "innate ideas," concedes, as so many
philosophers of the same school have done since, that this
native knowledge is only implicit and requires definite
experiences to elicit it.   Thus, in his notes on the Programme of Regius, he expressly compares these innate
notions or ideas with the nobility which is characteristic
of certain ancient stocks, or with diseases, such as gout or
gravel, which are said to be "innate" in certain families,
not "because the infants of those families suffer from these
diseases in their mother's womb, but because they are
born with a certain disposition or tendency to contract
them."   Here Descartes seems to have been on the very
point of stumbling on the principle of heredity which, in
the hands of recent physiologists and psychologists, has
done so much towards reconciling rival theories on the

K

nature and origin of knowledge and clearing up many of
the difficulties which attach to this branch of speculation.
It must be confessed, however, that in his better-known
works he often employs unguarded and unexplained expressions which might easily suggest the crude form of the
à priori theory attacked by Locke. Still more is this
the case with other authors, such as Lord Herbert of
Cherbury and Dr. Ralph Cudworth, whose works were in
general circulation at the time when Locke was com-
posing his *Essay*. Lord Herbert, though indeed he
acknowledges that " common notions" (the expression by
which he designates *à priori* principles) require an object to
elicit them into consciousness, seems invariably to regard
them as ready-made ideas implanted in the human mind
from its very origin. They are given by an independent
faculty, Natural Instinct, which is to be distinguished from
Internal Sense, External Sense, and Reasoning ("Discur-
sus"), the sources of our other ideas. They are to be found
in every man, and universal consent is the main criterion
by which they are to be discriminated. In fact, there can
be no doubt that the dogma of Innate Ideas and Innate
Principles, in the form attacked by Locke, was a natural,
if not the legitimate, interpretation of much of the philosophical teaching of the time, and that it was probably
the form in which that teaching was popularly understood. It lay, moreover, as Locke's phrase is, along the
" common road," which was travelled by the majority of
men who cared about speculative subjects at all, and from
which it was novel, and therefore dangerous, to diverge.

The most effective, perhaps, of Locke's arguments
against this doctrine is his challenge to the advocates of
Innate Principles to produce them, and show what and
how many they are. Did men find such innate proposi-

tions stamped on their minds, nothing could be more easy than this. "There could be no more doubt about their number than there is about the number of our fingers ; and 'tis like, then, every system would be ready to give them us by tale." Now "'tis enough to make one suspect that the supposition of such innate principles is but an opinion taken up at random ; since those who talk so confidently of them are so sparing to tell us which they are." (Bk. I., ch. iii., § 14.) The great majority, indeed, of those who maintain the existence of innate principles and ideas attempt no enumeration of them. Those who do attempt such an enumeration differ in the lists which they draw up, and, moreover, as Locke shows in the case of the five practical principles of Lord Herbert of Cherbury, give no sufficient reason why many other propositions, which they regard as secondary and derived, should not be admitted to the same rank with the so-called innate principles, which they assume to be primary and independent. Locke is here treading on safer ground than in many of his other criticisms. The fact is that it is impossible clearly to discriminate between those propositions which are axiomatic and those which are derived—or, in the language of the theory which Locke is combating, between those which are innate and those which are adventitious. Race, temperament, mental capacity, habit, education, produce such differences between man and man that a proposition which to one man appears self-evident and unquestionable will by another be admitted only after considerable hesitation, while a third will regard it as doubtful, or even false. Especially is this the case, as Locke does not fail to point out, with many of the principles of religion and morals, which have now been received by so constant a tradition in most civilized nations that they have come to be regarded as independent of reason, and, if not "ingraven on the mind" from its birth, at least exempt from discussion and criticism. The circumstance, however, that they are not universally acknowledged shows that to mankind in general, at any rate, they are not axiomatic, and that, however clear and convincing the reasons for them may be, at all events those reasons require to be stated. It was this determined and vigorous protest against multiplying assumptions and attempting to withdraw a vast mass of propositions, both speculative and practical, from the control and revision of reason that, perhaps, constituted the most distinctive and valuable part of Locke's teaching.

Having cleared from his path the theory of Innate Principles, Locke proceeds, in the Second Book, to inquire how the mind comes to be furnished with its knowledge. Availing himself of a metaphor which had been commonly employed by the Stoics, but which reaches as far back as Aristotle and Plato, and even as Æschylus, he compares the mind to "white paper, void of all characters, without any ideas," and then asks :—

"Whence comes it by that vast store, which the busy and boundless Fancy of Man has painted on it, with an almost endless variety? Whence has it all the materials of Reason and Knowledge? To this I answer in one word, From *Experience:* In that all our knowledge is founded; and from that it ultimately derives itself. Our observation employed either about external or sensible objects, or about the internal operations of our minds perceived and reflected on by our selves, is that which supplies our Understandings with all the materials of thinking. These two are the Fountains of Knowledge from which all the ideas we have. or can naturally have, do spring."

"First, our Senses, conversant about particular sensible objects, do convey into the mind several distinct perceptions of things, according to those various ways in which those objects do affect them. And thus we come by those ideas we have of Yellow, White, Heat, Cold, Soft, Hard, Bitter, Sweet, and all those which we call Sensible Qualities, which when I say the senses convey into the mind, I mean they from external objects convey into the mind what produces there those Perceptions. This great source of most of the Ideas we have, depending wholly upon our senses, and derived by them to the Understanding, I call SENSATION."

"Secondly, the other Fountain, from which Experience furnisheth the Understanding with Ideas, is the Perception of the operations of our own minds within us, as it is employed about the ideas it has got; which operations, when the soul comes to reflect on and consider, do furnish the Understanding with another set of ideas which could not be had from things without; and such are Perception, Thinking, Doubting, Believing, Reasoning, Knowing, Willing, and all the different actings of our own minds, which we being conscious of, and observing in our selves, do from these receive into our Understandings as distinct ideas as we do from bodies affecting our senses. This source of ideas every man has wholly in himself. And though it be not sense, as having nothing to do with external objects, yet it is very like it, and might properly enough be called Internal Sense. But as I call the other *Sensation*, so I call this REFLECTION, the ideas it affords being such only as the mind gets by reflecting on its own operations within itself. By Reflection, then, in the following part of this Discourse, I would be understood to mean that notice which the mind takes of its own operations and the manner of them, by reason whereof there come to be Ideas of these operations in the Understanding. These two, I say, namely, external material things, as the objects of Sensation, and the operations of our own minds within, as the objects of Reflection, are to me the only originals from whence all our ideas take their beginning. The term operations here I use in a large sense, as comprehending not barely the actions of the mind about its ideas, but some sort of passions arising sometimes from them, such as is the satisfaction or uneasiness arising from any thought."

"The Understanding seems to me not to have the least glimmering of any ideas which it doth not receive from one of these two. External objects furnish the mind with the ideas of sensible qualities, which are all those different perceptions they produce in us; and the mind furnishes the Understanding with ideas of its own operations." (Bk. II., ch. i., §§ 2—5.)

In deriving our knowledge from two distinct sources, Sensation and Reflection, Locke is advancing a position altogether different from that of what is properly called the Sensationalist school of philosophers. Gassendi and Hobbes before him, Condillac and Helvétius after him, found the ultimate source of all our knowledge in the impressions of sense. The emphatic words of Hobbes, standing in the forefront of the *Leviathan*, are :—" The original of all the thoughts of men is that which we call Sense, for there is no conception in a man's mind which hath not at first, totally or by parts, been begotten upon the organs of sense." And Condillac, aiming at a theory still more simple, derives from sensations not only all our knowledge but all our faculties. "The other fountain," then, of Locke has, we must recollect, a peculiar significance as distinguishing his psychology from that of the sensationalist writers who preceded and who followed him. His theory of the origin of knowledge may fairly be called an experiential, but it cannot with any truth be called a sensationalist theory.

The rest of the Second Book of the *Essay* is mainly taken up with the attempt to enumerate our simple ideas of Sensation and Reflection, and to resolve into them our other ideas, however complex. To follow Locke into these details would be to re-write the *Essay*. I propose simply to direct the attention of the reader to a few salient points.

Of " Simple Ideas of Sensation," some " come into our minds by one Sense only." Such are the various colours, sounds, tastes, and smells, Heat and Cold, and the sensation of Resistance or Impenetrability, which Locke denominates Solidity. "The Ideas we get by more than one sense are of Space or Extension, Figure, Rest, and Motion."

The "Simple Ideas of Reflection," which the mind acquires, when "it turns its view inward upon itself, and observes its own actions about those ideas it has received from without," are mainly two, namely, Perception or Thinking, and Volition or Willing.

"There be other simple ideas, which convey themselves into the mind by all the ways of Sensation and Reflection, namely, Pleasure or Delight, Pain or Uneasiness, Power, Existence, Unity. (Bk. II., ch. vii., § 1.)

"These simple ideas, the materials of all our knowledge, are suggested and furnished to the mind only by those two ways above mentioned, namely Sensation and Reflection. When the Understanding is once stored with these simple ideas, it has the power to repeat, compare, and unite them, even to an almost infinite variety, and so can make at pleasure new complex ideas. But it is not in the power of the most exalted Wit or enlarged Understanding, by any quickness or variety of thoughts, to invent or frame one new simple idea in the mind, not taken in by the ways before mentioned. Nor can any force of the Understanding destroy those that are there : the dominion of man, in this little world of his own understanding, being much what the same as it is in the great world of visible things, wherein his power, however managed by art and skill, reaches no farther than to compound and divide the materials that are made to his hand, but can do nothing towards the making the least particle of new

matter or destroying one atom of what is already in being.
The same inability will every one find in himself, who shall go
about to fashion in his Understanding any simple idea, not received in by his senses from external objects or by reflection
from the operations of his own mind about them." (Bk. II.
ch. ii., § 2.)

In the reception of these simple ideas, Locke regards
the mind as merely passive. It can no more refuse to
have them, alter or blot them out, than a mirror can
refuse to receive, alter, or obliterate the images reflected
on it. The Understanding, before the entrance of simple
ideas, is like a dark room, and external and internal sensation are the windows by which light is let in. But when
the light has once penetrated into this dark recess, the
Understanding has an almost unlimited power of modify-
ing and transforming it. It can create complex ideas,
and that in an infinite variety, out of its simple ideas, and
this it does chiefly by combining, comparing, and sepa-
rating them.

"This shows man's power, and its way of operation, to be
much what the same in the material and intellectual world.
For the materials in both being such as he has no power over,
either to make or destroy, all that man can do is either to unite
them together, or to set them by one another, or wholly separate
them." (Bk. II., ch. xii., § 1.)

The complex ideas are classified under three heads,
modes, which may be either simple or mixed, substances,
and relations. Here, however, my analysis must stop, and
I must content myself with giving a few examples of the
manner in which Locke attempts to resolve "complex
ideas" into "simple" ones.

The idea of Infinity, to take one of his most celebrated
resolutions, is merely a simple mode of Quantity, as Im-

mensity is a simple mode of Space, and Eternity of Duration. All alike are negative ideas, arising whenever we allow the mind " an endless progression of thought," without any effort to arrest it. " How often soever " a man doubles an unit of space, be it a " mile, or diameter of the earth, or of the *Orbis Magnus*," or any otherwise multiplies it, "he finds that, after he has continued this doubling in his thoughts and enlarged his idea as much as he pleases, he has no more reason to stop, nor is one jot nearer the end of such addition, than he was at first setting out; the power of enlarging his idea of Space by farther additions remaining still the same, he hence takes idea of infinite space." (Bk. II., ch. xvii., § 3.)

With the idea of " Substance " Locke is fairly baffled. If we examine our idea of a horse, a man, a piece of gold, &c., we are able to resolve it into a number of simple ideas, such as extension, figure, solidity, weight, colour, &c., co-existing together. But, according to Locke, who, in this respect, was merely following in the track of the generally received philosophy of his time, there is, in addition to all these qualities, a *substratum* in which they inhere, or, to use his own language, " wherein they do subsist, and from which they do result." Now of the various qualities we can form a clear idea and give a more or less intelligible account. But can we form a clear idea or give an intelligible account of the substratum? Locke here is bold enough to break off from the orthodox doctrine of the time, and confess candidly that we cannot. The idea of this Substratum or Substance is a "confused idea of something to which the qualities belong, and in which they subsist." The name Substance denotes a Support, " though it be certain we have no clear or distinct idea of that thing we suppose a support."

"So that if any one will examine himself concerning his notion of pure Substance in general, he will find he has no other idea of it at all but only a supposition of he knows not what Support of such qualities which are capable of producing simple ideas in us; which qualities are commonly called Accidents. If any one should be asked what is the subject wherein Colour or Weight inheres, he would have nothing to say but the solid extended parts. And if he were demanded what is it that Solidity and Extension inhere in, he would not be in a much better case than the Indian who, saying that the world was supported by a great elephant, was asked what the elephant rested on? To which his answer was, a great tortoise. But, being again pressed to know what gave support to the broad-backed tortoise, replied, something, he knew not what. And thus here, as in all other cases, where we use words without having clear and distinct ideas, we talk like children; who, being questioned what such a thing is, which they know not, readily give this satisfactory answer, That it is something; which in truth signifies no more, when so used, either by children or men, but that they know not what, and that the thing they pretend to know and talk of is what they have no distinct idea of at all, and so are perfectly ignorant of it and in the dark." (Bk. II., ch. xxiii., § 2.)

No wonder that the next step in philosophy was to get rid altogether of this "something, we know not what." For, if we know not what it is, how do we know that it exists, and is not a mere fiction of the Schools? This step was taken by Berkeley, as respects matter, and by Hume the same negative criticism which Berkeley confines to matter was boldly, and, as it seems to me, far less successfully and legitimately extended to mind. Indeed, were it not for his express assurance to the contrary, we should often be tempted to think that Locke himself regarded this distinction of Substance and Accident, so far, at least, as it affects Matter and its attributes, as untenable, and was anxious to insinuate a doubt as to the very existence of the " unknown somewhat."

In this chapter, Locke maintains that there is no more difficulty, if indeed so much, in the notion of immaterial spirit as of body. "Our idea of Body, as I think, is an extended solid substance, capable of communicating motion by impulse; and our idea of our Soul, as an immaterial Spirit, is of a substance that thinks, and has a power of exciting motion in body by Will or Thought." (§ 22.) Now, it is " no more a contradiction that Thinking should exist separate and independent from Solidity, than it is a contradiction that Solidity should exist separate and independent from Thinking, they being both but simple ideas independent one from another. And, having as clear and distinct ideas in us of Thinking as of Solidity, I know not why we may not as well allow a thinking thing without solidity, that is immaterial, to exist, as a solid thing without thinking, that is matter, to exist; especially since it is no harder to conceive how Thinking should exist without Matter, than how Matter should think." (§ 32.)

In the Fourth Book (ch. iii., § 6), however, he gave great scandal by suggesting the possibility that Matter might think, that it was not much more repugnant to our conceptions that God might, if he pleased, " superadd to Matter a Faculty of Thinking, than that he should superadd to it another substance with a faculty of thinking." At the same time, he regarded it as no less than a contradiction to suppose that Matter, " which is evidently in its own nature void of sense and thought," should be the " eternal first thinking Being," or God Himself; and, in his First Letter to the Bishop of Worcester, he grants that *in us* (as distinguished from the lower animals) it is, in the highest degree, probable that the " thinking substance" is immaterial. Materialism, therefore, as ordinarily understood, is certainly no part of Locke's system.

In discussing the idea of Substance, Locke seems generally to be thinking more of Matter than Mind. But, in an early part of the *Essay* (Bk. II., ch. xiii., § 18), he very rightly begs those who talk so much of Substance "to consider whether applying it, as they do, to the infinite incomprehensible God, to finite Spirit, and to Body, it be in the same sense, and whether it stands for the same idea, when each of those three so different beings are called Substances." As applied respectively to Matter and to Mind (whether finite or infinite), it appears to me that the word Substance assumes a very different meaning, and that the absurdities which it is possible to fix on the distinction between Matter and its attributes by no means extend to the distinction between Mind and its operations. For an union of certain forces or powers affecting our organisms in certain ways seems to exhaust our conception of external objects (the notion of externality, I conceive, being quite independent of that of the Substrate "matter"), but no similar enumeration of mental acts and feelings seems adequately to take the place of that "Self," or "I," of which we regard these as merely phases and modifications. It would much conduce to clearness in philosophical discussions if, at least amongst those who admit the dualism of matter and mind, the word Substance, whenever applied to incorporeal objects, were replaced by the word Mind, and, whenever applied to corporeal objects, by the word Matter.

The Second Book closes, in the Fourth and subsequent editions, with a short but very interesting Chapter on the "Association of Ideas." The student of Mental Philosophy will find it instructive to compare this Chapter with the previous account given by Hobbes (*Human Nature*, ch. iv. ; *Leviathan*, Pt. I., ch. iii.), and the subsequent account given by Hume (*Human Nature*, Pt. I., § 4 ; *Essays on Human Understanding*, § 3), of the same phenomena.   Locke appears to have been the first author to use the exact[1] expression " Association of Ideas," and it is curious to find in this chapter (§ 5) the word " inseparable," so familiar to the readers of recent works on psychology, already applied to designate certain kinds of association.   Some ideas, indeed, have, he says, a natural correspondence, but others, that " in themselves are not at all of kin," " come to be so united in some men's minds that one no sooner at any time comes into the understanding than the whole Gang, always inseparable, show themselves together."

The following passage on what may be called the associations of antipathy affords a good instance of Locke's power of homely and apposite illustration :—

" Many children imputing the pain they endured at school to their books they were corrected for, so join those ideas together, that a book becomes their aversion, and they are never reconciled to the study and use of them all their lives after; and thus reading becomes a torment to them, which otherwise possibly they might have made the great pleasure of their lives.   There are rooms convenient enough, that some men cannot study in, and fashions of vessels, which though never so clean and commodious, they cannot drink out of, and that by reason of some accidental ideas which are annexed to them and make them

[1] Sir W. Hamilton refers to La Chambre (*Système de l'Ame :* Paris, 1664) as having anticipated Locke in the use of this expression. In Liv. IV., ch. ii., art. 9, La Chambre speaks of " l' Union et la Liaison des Images," but I cannot find that he approaches any nearer to the now established phraseology.

offensive. And who is there that hath not observed some man to flag at the appearance or in the company of some certain person not otherwise superior to him, but because, having once on some occasion got the ascendant, the idea of authority and distance goes along with that of the person, and he that has been thus subjected is not able to separate them."

Had Locke's *Essay* ended with the Second Book, we should hardly have detected in it any incompleteness. It might have been regarded as an analytical work on the nature and origin of our ideas, or, in other words, on the elements of our knowledge. There are, however, a third and fourth book—the former treating "Of Words," the latter "Of Knowledge and Opinion." Locke's notion appears to have been that, after treating of "Ideas," mainly as regarded in themselves, it was desirable to consider them as combined in Judgments or Propositions, and to estimate the various degrees of assent which we give or ought to give to such judgments, when formed. The Fourth Book thus, to a certain extent, takes the place, and was probably designed to take the place, of the Logic of the Schools. " But," to quote Locke's own language in the Abstract of the *Essay*, " when I came a little nearer to consider the nature and manner of human knowledge, I found it had so much to do with propositions, and that words, either by custom or necessity, were so mixed with it, that it was impossible to discourse of knowledge with that clearness we should, without saying something first of words and language."

The three last Chapters of the Third Book are remarkable for their sound sense, and may still be read with the greatest advantage by all who wish to be put on their guard against the delusions produced by misleading or inadequate language—those " Idola Fori " which Bacon describes as the most troublesome of the phantoms which beset the mind in its search for truth. Some of the best and freshest of Locke's thoughts, indeed, are to be found in this book, and specially in the less technical parts of it.

The Fourth Book, under the head of Knowledge, treats of a great variety of interesting topics : of the nature of knowledge, its degrees, its extent, and reality ; of the truth and certainty of Universal Propositions ; of the logical axioms, or laws of thought ; of the evidence for the existence of a God ; of Faith and Reason ; of the Degrees of Assent ; of Enthusiasm ; of Error. Into these attractive regions it is impossible that I can follow my author, but the reader who wishes to see examples of Locke's strong practical sense and, at the same time, to understand the popularity so soon and so constantly accorded to the *Essay*, should make acquaintance at least with the four chapters last named.

From the task of description I now pass to that of criticism, though this must be confined within still narrower limits than the former, and indeed, amongst the multiplicity of subjects which invite attention, I must confine myself to one only : the account of the ultimate origin of our knowledge, which forms the main subject of the *Essay*.

Locke, as we have seen, derived all our knowledge from Experience. But experience, with him, was simply the experience of the individual. In order to acquire this experience, it was indeed necessary that we should have certain " inherent faculties." But of these " faculties " he gives no other account than that God has " furnished " or " endued " us with them. Thus, the *Deus ex machina* was as much an acknowledged necessity in the philosophy of Locke, and was, in fact, almost as frequently invoked, as in that of his antagonists. Is there any natural account to be given of the way in which we come to have these "faculties," of the extraordinary facility we possess of acquiring simple and forming complex ideas, is a question which he appears never to have put to himself. Inquiries of this kind, however, we must recollect were foreign to the men of his generation, and, in fact, have only recently become a recognized branch of mental philosophy. Hence it was that his system left so much unexplained. Not only the very circumstance that we have "inherent faculties" at all, but the wide differences of natural capacity which we observe between one man or race and another, and the very early period at which there spring up in the mind such notions as those of space, time, equality, causality, and the like, are amongst the many difficulties which Locke's theory, in its bare and unqualified form, fails satisfactorily to answer. It was thus comparatively easy for Kant to show that the problem of the origin of knowledge could not be left where Locke had left it; that our *à posteriori* experiences presuppose and are only intelligible through certain *à priori* perceptions and conceptions which the mind itself imposes upon them; or, to use more accurate language, through certain *à priori* elements in our perceptions and conceptions, which the mind contributes from itself. Thus the child appears, as soon as it is capable of recognizing any source of its impressions, to regard an object as situated in space, an event as happening in time, circumstances which have occurred together as likely to occur together again. But Kant's own account was defective in leaving this *à priori* element of our knowledge unexplained, or, at least, in attempting no explanation of it. The mind, according to him, is possessed of certain Forms and Categories, which shape and co-ordinate the impressions received from the external world, being as necessary to the acquisition of experience, as experience is necessary to eliciting them into consciousness. But here his analysis ends. He does not ask how the mind comes to be possessed of these Forms and Categories, nor does he satisfactorily determine the precise relation in which they stand to the empirical elements of knowledge. When studying his philosophy, we seem indeed to be once more receding to the mysterious region of Innate Ideas. But the mystery is removed at least several stages back, if we apply to the solution of these mental problems the principle of Heredity, which has recently been found so potent in clearing up many of the difficulties connected with external nature. What are the "Innate Ideas" of the older philosophers, or the Forms and Categories of Kant, but certain *tendencies* of the mind to group phenomena, the "fleeting objects of sense," under certain relations and regard them under certain aspects? And why should these tendencies be accounted for in any other way than that by which we are accustomed to account for the tendency of an animal or plant, belonging to any particular species, to exhibit, as it developes, the physical characteristics of the species to which it belongs? The existence of the various mental tendencies and aptitudes, so far as the individual is concerned, is, in fact, to be explained by the principle of hereditary transmission. But how have these tendencies and aptitudes come to be formed in the race? The most scientific answer is that which, following the analogy of the theory now so widely admitted with respect to the physical structure of animals and plants, assigns their formation to

L

the continuous operation, through a long series of ages, of causes acting uniformly, or almost uniformly, in the same direction—in one word, of Evolution. This explanation may have its difficulties, but it is at any rate an attempt at a natural explanation where no other such attempt exists, and it has the merit of falling in with the explanations of corresponding phenomena now most generally accepted amongst scientific men in other departments of knowledge.

According to this theory, there is both an *à priori* and an *à posteriori* element in our knowledge, or, to speak more accurately, there are both *à priori* and *à posteriori* conditions of our knowing, the *à posteriori* condition being, as in all systems, individual experience, the *à priori* condition being inherited mental aptitudes, which, as a rule, become more and more marked and persistent with each successive transmission. Now Locke lays stress simply upon the *à posteriori* condition, though he recognizes a certain kind of *à priori* condition in our " natural faculties " and the simple ideas furnished by reflecting on their operations. The very important condition, however, of inherited aptitudes facilitating the formation of certain general conceptions concurrently or almost concurrently with the presentation of individual experiences did not occur to him as an element in the solution of the problem he had undertaken to answer, nor, in that stage of speculation, could it well have done so. His peculiar contribution to the task of solving this question consisted in his skilful and popular delineation of the *à posteriori* element in knowledge, and in his masterly exposure of the insufficiency of the account of the *à priori* element, as then commonly given. Locke's own theory was afterwards strained by Hume and

Hartley, and still more by his professed followers in France, such as Condillac and Helvétius, till at last, in the opinion of most competent judges, it snapped asunder. Then, under the massive, though often partial and obscure, treatment of Kant, came the rehabilitation of the *à priori* side of knowledge. In recent times, mainly by aid of the light thrown on it from other branches of inquiry, a more thorough and scientific treatment of psychology has done much, as I conceive, towards completing and reconciling the two divergent theories which at one time seemed hopelessly to divide the world of philosophic thinkers. And yet, as it appears to me, the ultimate mystery which surrounds the beginnings of intellectual life on the globe has by no means been removed.

As closely connected with this general criticism of Locke's system, or rather as presenting the defects just criticized under another form, I may notice the tendency of the *Essay* to bring into undue prominence the passive receptivities of the Mind, and to ignore its activity and spontaneity. The metaphor of the *tabula rasa*, the sheet of " white paper," once admitted, exercises a warping influence over the whole work. The author is so busied with the variety of impressions from without, that he seems sometimes almost to ignore the reaction of the mind from within. And yet this one-sidedness of Locke's conception of mind may easily be exaggerated. " When the Understanding is once stored with simple ideas, it has the power to repeat, compare, and unite them, even to an almost infinite variety, and so can make at pleasure new complex ideas." (Bk. II., ch. ii., § 2.) Moreover, amongst the simple ideas themselves are the ideas of Reflection, " being such as the mind gets by reflecting on its own operations." The system, in fact, assumes an

almost ceaseless activity of mind, after the simple ideas
of sensation have once entered it. But where it fails is in
not recognizing that mental reaction which is essential
to the formation of even the simple ideas of sensation
themselves, as well as that spontaneous activity of mind
which often seems to assert itself independently of the
application of any stimulus from without. Here again
a more scientific psychology than was possible in Locke's
day comes to our aid, and shows, as is done by Mr.
Bain and other recent writers, that the nerves, stored with
energy, often discharge themselves of their own accord,
and that movement is at least as much an original factor in
animal life as is sensation, while sometimes it even precedes
it in time. Had the constant interaction of mental
activity and mental receptivity, producing a compound in
which it is often almost impossible to disentangle the
elements, been duly recognized by Locke, it would certainly
have made his philosophy less simple, but it would have
made it more true to facts. Physiology, however, was in his
days in far too backward a state itself to throw much
light upon Psychology. And the reaction against the
prevailing doctrine of Innate Ideas naturally led to a
system in which the influences of external circumstances,
of education and habit, were exaggerated at the expense
of the native powers, or as they might more appropriately
be called the inherited aptitudes, and the spontaneous
activity of the mind.

Here, tempting as it is to follow my author along the
many tracks of psychological, metaphysical, and logical
discussion which he always pursues with sagacity, candour,
and good sense, if not always with the consistency and
profundity which we should require from later writers, my
criticism must necessarily end.

Before, however, finally dismissing the *Essay*, I must pause to ask what was the main work in the history of philosophy and thought which it accomplished. Many of its individual doctrines, doubtless, could not now be defended against the attacks of hostile criticism, and some even of those which are true in the main, are inadequate or one-sided. But its excellence lies in its tone, its language, its method, its general drift, its multiplicity of topics, the direction which it gave to the thoughts and studies of reflecting men for many generations subsequent to its appearance. Of the tone of candour and open-mindedness which pervades it, of the unscholastic and agreeable form in which it is written, and of the great variety of interesting topics which it starts, I have spoken already. Its method, though not absolutely new, even in modern times, for it is at least, to some extent, the method of Descartes, if not, in a smaller degeee, of Hobbes and Gassendi, was still not common at the time of its appear, ance. Instead of stating a series of preconceived opinions-or of dogmas borrowed from some dominant school, in a systematic form, Locke sets to work to examine the structure of his own mind, and to analyze into their elements the ideas which he finds there. This, the *introspective* method, as it has been called, though undoubtedly imperfect, for it requires to be supplemented by the study of the minds of other men, if not of the lower animals, as made known by their acts, and words, and history, is yet a great advance on the purely *à priori*, and often fanciful, methods which preceded it. Nor do we fail to find in the *Essay* some employment of that *comparative* method to which I have just alluded : witness the constant references to children and savages in the First Book, and the stress which is laid on the variety of moral sentiment existing amongst mankind. This inductive treatment of philosophical problems, mainly introspective, but in some measure also comparative, which was extremely rare in Locke's time, became almost universal afterwards. Closely connected with the method of the book is its general purport. By turning the mind inwards upon itself, and "making it its own object," Locke surmises that all its ideas come either from without or from experience of its own operations. He finds, on examination and analysis, no ideas which cannot be referred to one or other of these two sources. The single word "experience" includes them both, and furnishes us with a good expression for marking the general drift of his philosophy. It was pre-eminently a philosophy of experience, both in its method and in its results. It accepts nothing on authority, no foregone conclusions, no data from other sciences. It digs, as it were, into the mind, detaches the ore, analyzes it, and asks how the various constituents came there. The analytical and psychological direction thus given to philosophy by Locke was followed by most of the philosophical writers of the eighteenth century. However divergent in other respects, Hume and Berkeley, Hartley and Reid, the French Sensationalists, Kant, all commence their investigations by inquiring into the constitution, the capacities, and the limits of the Human Mind. Nor can any system of speculation be constructed on a sound basis, which has neglected to dig about the foundations of human knowledge, to ascertain what our thoughts can and what they cannot compass, and what are the varying degrees of assurance with which the various classes of propositions may be accepted by us. Two cautions, indeed, are necessary in applying this procedure. We must never forget that the mind is constantly

in contact with external nature, and that therefore a constant action and reaction is taking place between them;
and we must never omit to base our inductions on an
examination of other minds as well as our own, bringing
into the account, as far as possible, every type and grade
of mental development.

It was not, however, only its general spirit and direction which Locke impressed on the philosophy of the
eighteenth century. He may almost be said to have re-
created that philosophy. There is hardly a single French
or English writer (and we may add Kant) down to the
time of Dugald Stewart, or even of Cousin, Hamilton, and
J. S. Mill, who does not profess either to develope
Locke's system, or to supplement, or to criticize it. Followers, antagonists, and critics alike, seem to assume on
the part of the reader a knowledge of the *Essay on the
Human Understanding,* and to make that the starting-
point of their own speculations. The office which Bacon
assigns to himself with reference to knowledge generally
might well have been claimed by Locke with reference to
the science of mind. Both of them did far more than
merely play the part of a herald, but of both alike it was
emphatically true that they "rang the bell to call the other
wits together."

CHAPTER IX.

In the *Essay on the Human Understanding*, Bk. IV.,
ch. x., Locke attempts to prove the existence of a God,
which, though God has given us no innate idea of Himself,
he regards as "the most obvious truth that reason dis-
cerns," and as resting on evidence equal to mathematical
certainty. Morality is, he maintains, entirely based upon
the Will of God. If there were no God, there would,
for him, be no morality, and this is the reason of his
denying to Atheists the protection of the State. In the
chapter on the Existence of God he says expressly that
this truth is so fundamental that "all genuine morality
depends thereon," and almost at the beginning of the
Essay (Bk. I., ch. iii., § 6), while acknowledging that
"several moral rules may receive from mankind a very
general approbation, without either knowing or admitting
the true ground of morality," he maintains that such true
ground "can only be the Will and Law of a God, who sees
men in the dark, has in his hand rewards and punishments, and power enough to call to account the proudest
offender." Again, "the Rule prescribed by God is the true
and only measure of Virtue." But how are we to ascer-

tain this rule? " God has by an inseparable connexion joined Virtue and Public Happiness together," and, hence, we have only to ascertain, by the use of the natural reason, what on the whole conduces most to the public welfare, in order to know the Divine Will. The rules, when arrived at, have a "moral and eternal obligation," and are enforced by fear of " the Hell God has ordained for the punishment of those that transgress them."

This form of Utilitarianism, resting on a theological basis and enforced by theological sanctions, is precisely that which afterwards became so popular and excited so much attention, when adopted in the well-known work of Paley. According to this system, we do what is right simply because God commands it, and because He will punish us if we disobey His orders. " By the fault is the rod, and with the transgression a fire ready to punish it." But, notwithstanding the divine origin and the divine sanction of morality, its measure and test are purely human. Each man is required by the Law of God to do all the good and prevent all the evil that he can, and, as good and evil are resolved into pleasure and pain, the ultimate test of virtue or moral conduct comes to be its conduciveness to promote the pleasures and avert the pains of mankind. Bentham, whose ethical system, it may be noticed, differed mainly from that of Locke and Paley by not being based on a theological foundation, extends the scope of morality to all sentient creatures, capable of pleasure and pain.

I shall not here criticize Locke's theory so far as it is common to other utilitarian systems of ethics, but shall simply content myself with pointing out that its influence on subsequent writers has seldom, if ever, been sufficiently recognized. The theological foundation, however, on which

it rests, and which is peculiar among the more prominent
moralists of modern times to Locke and Paley, is open to
an objection so grave and obvious, that it is curious it did
not occur to the authors themselves.   If what is right and
wrong, good and evil, depends solely on the Will of God,
how can we speak of God Himself as good?   Goodness,
as one of the Divine attributes, would then simply mean
the conformity of God to His own Will.   An elder contemporary of Locke, Ralph Cudworth, so clearly saw the
difficulties and contradictions involved in this view of the
nature and origin of morality, that he devotes a considerable portion of his *Treatise concerning Eternal and Immutable Morality* (which, however, was not published till
1731) to its refutation.   And, possibly, Locke himself
may have been conscious of some inconsistency between
this theory (the ordinary one amongst the vulgar, though
a comparatively rare one amongst philosophers) and the
attribution of goodness to God.   For, in his chapter on
our knowledge of the existence of God, he never expressly mentions the attribute of goodness as pertaining
to the Divine Nature, though in other parts of the *Essay*
it must be acknowledged that he incidentally does so.
Moralists and philosophical theologians have generally
escaped the difficulties of Locke's theory by making right
or moral goodness depend not on the Will but on the
Nature of God, or else by regarding it as an ultimate fact,
incapable of explanation, or, lastly, by resolving it into
the idea of happiness or pleasure, which itself is then
regarded as an ultimate fact in the constitution of sentient
beings.

Two other characteristic doctrines of Locke's ethical
system ought here to be mentioned, though it is impossible,
within the space at my command, to discuss them.   One

is that morality is a science capable of demonstration. The other, which is elaborately set out in the chapter on Power in the *Essay* (Bk. II., ch. xxi.), is that, though the Agent is free to act as he wills, the Will itself is invariably determined by motives. This solution of the well-worn controversy on the Freedom of the Will is almost identical with that offered by Hobbes before and by Hume afterwards, and is usually known as Determinism.

We have seen that the main sanctions of morality, with Locke, are the rewards and punishments of a future state. But how are we assured of future existence? Only by Revelation. " Good and wise men," indeed, "have always been willing to believe that the soul was immortal," but "though the Light of Nature gave some obscure glimmering, some uncertain hopes of a future state, yet Human Reason could attain to no clearness, no certainty about it, but it was Jesus Christ alone who brought life and immortality to light through the gospel." (Third Letter to the Bp. of Worcester). But, if the main sanctions of morality are those of a future state, and if it is Christians alone who feel anything approaching to an assurance of such a state, surely morality must come with somewhat weak credentials to the rest of mankind.   And Locke doubtless believed this to be the case.   But, then, if this be so, Christians ought to be prepared to tolerate a much lower morality than their own in dealing with men of other faiths—one of the many inconvenient consequences which result from founding morality on a theological basis.

Under the head of Locke's theological writings may be included the *Treatise on the Reasonableness of Christianity*

with the two *Vindications* of it, the *Essays on Toleration*,
and the *Commentaries on some of the Epistles of St.
Paul.* The *Reasonableness of Christianity* was published
in 1695, and may be taken as expressing Locke's most
matured opinions on the questions of which it treats, though,
in reading it, we must always bear in mind the caution
and reticence which any writer of that time, who diverged
from the strict path of orthodoxy, was obliged to observe.
There can be no doubt that his object in this work was to
commend what he regarded as the fundamental truths of
Christianity to the attention of reflecting men, and to
vindicate to the Christian religion what he conceived to be
its legitimate influence over mankind. But, in trying to
effect this his main object, he seems also to have
wished to correct what he regarded as certain popular
errors, and to bring back Christianity to the norm
of the Scriptures, instead of implicitly following the
Fathers, the Councils, and the received theology of the
Churches and the Schools. He attempted, he tells us, to
clear his mind of all preconceived notions, and, following
the lead of the Scriptures, of which he assumed the infallibility, to see whither they would lead him. We may
certainly trust his own assertion that he had no thoughts of
writing in the interest of any particular party, though, at
the same time, it was evidently his aim to extract from
the Scriptures a theory as much as possible in accordance
with the requirements of human reason, or, in other words,
to reconcile the divine light with the natural light of
man. The main results at which he arrived may be stated
very briefly, as follows. Adam had been created immortal,
but, by falling from the state of perfect obedience, "he
lost paradise, wherein was tranquillity and the tree of life,
that is he lost bliss and immortality." " In Adam all

die," and hence all his descendants are mortal. But this
sentence is to be taken in its literal sense, and not in the
signification that " every one descended of him deserves
endless torment in hell-fire." For it seems "a strange way
of understanding a law, which requires the plainest and
directest words, that by death should be meant eternal life
in misery." Much less can death be interpreted as a
necessity of continual sinning. " Can the righteous God
be supposed, as a punishment of our sin, wherewith He is
displeased, to put man under the necessity of sinning con-
tinually, and so multiplying the provocation ? " Here it
will be seen Locke strikes at the root of the doctrines of
the taint and guilt of original sin, doctrines which had
long been stoutly opposed by the Arminians or Remonstrants with whom he had associated in Holland. But
though it would have been an injustice to condemn men,
for the fault of another, to a state of misery "worse than
non-being," it was no wrong to deprive them of that to
which they had no right, the exceptional condition of immortality. Adam's sin then subjected all men to death.
But in Christ they have again been made alive, and " the
life which Jesus Christ restores to all men, is that life
which they receive again at the resurrection." Now the
conditions of our obtaining this gift are faith and repentance.
But repentance implies the doing works meet for repentance,
that is to say, leading a good life. And faith implies a
belief not only in the one invisible, eternal, omnipotent
God, but also in Jesus as the Messiah, who was born of a
virgin, rose again from the grave, and ascended into
heaven. When Christ came on earth, the minds of men
had become so far blinded by sense and lust and super-
stition that it required some visible and unmistakable
assertion of God's majesty and goodness to bring them

back to true notions of Him and of the Divine Law which He had set them. "Reason, speaking ever so clearly to the wise and virtuous, had never authority enough to prevail on the multitude." For the multitude were under the dominion of the priests, and "the priests, everywhere, to secure their empire, had excluded reason from having anything to do in religion." "In this state of darkness and error, in reference to the 'true God,' our Saviour found the world. But the clear revelation he brought with him dissipated this darkness, made the 'one invisible true God' known to the world ; and that with such evidence and energy, that polytheism and idolatry have nowhere been able to withstand it." And, as he revealed to mankind a clear knowledge of the one true God, so also he revealed to them a clear knowledge of their duty, which was equally wanting.

"Natural religion, in its full extent, was nowhere that I know taken care of by the force of natural reason. It should seem, by the little that has hitherto been done in it, that it is too hard a task for unassisted reason to establish morality in all its parts, upon its true foundation, with a clear and convincing light. And it is at least a surer and shorter way to the apprehensions of the vulgar and mass of mankind, that one manifestly sent from God, and coming with visible authority from him, should, as a king and law-maker, tell them their duties and require their obedience, than leave it to the long and sometimes intricate deductions of reason to be made out to them. Such trains of reasoning the greater part of mankind have neither leisure to weigh, nor, for want of education and use, skill to judge of. . . . . You may as soon hope to have all the day-labourers and tradesmen, the spinsters and dairy-maids, perfect mathematicians, as to have them perfect in ethics this way. Hearing plain commands is the sure and only course to bring them to obedience and practice. The greater part cannot learn, and therefore they must believe."

It is true that reason quickly apprehends and approves of these truths, when once delivered, but " native and original truth is not so easily wrought out of the mine, as we, who have it delivered already dug and fashioned into our hands, are apt to imagine ;" moreover, " experience shows that the knowledge of morality by mere natural light (how agreeable soever it be to it) makes but a slow progress and little advance in the world."

The evidence of Christ's mission is to be found in the miracles, the occurrence and the divine origin of which Locke, both here and in the paper on Miracles published among his Posthumous Works, appears to have thought it impossible to gain-say. " The miracles he did were so ordered by the divine providence and wisdom, that they never were nor could be denied by any of the enemies or opposers of Christianity." And " this plain matter of fact being granted, the truth of our Saviour's doctrine and mission unavoidably follows." But once acknowledge the truth of Christ's mission, and the rule of life is evident. " To one who is once persuaded that Jesus Christ was sent by God to be a King, and a Saviour of those who do believe in him, all his commands become principles ; there needs no other proof for the truth of what he says, but that he said it. And then there needs no more, but to read the inspired books, to be instructed ; all the duties of morality lie there clear, and plain, and easy to be understood."

This, then, is Locke's scheme of a plain and reasonable Christianity. " These are articles that the labouring and illiterate man may comprehend. This is a religion suited to vulgar capacities, and the state of mankind in this world, destined to labour and travail." " The writers and wranglers in religion," indeed, "fill it with niceties,

and dress it up with notions, which they make necessary
and fundamental parts of it, as if there were no way into
the church, but through the academy or lyceum," but the
religion which he had enunciated was, Locke conceived,
the religion of Christ and the Apostles, of the New Testament and of Common-Sense.

That Locke, though he had no respect for the dogmas
of the Church, never seriously questioned the supernatural
birth of Christ, the reality of the Christian miracles, or
the infallibility of the Scriptures, is abundantly evident.
On the last point his testimony is quite as emphatic as
on the two former.   In the *Reasonableness of Christianity*,
speaking of the writers of the Epistles, he says :—" These
holy writers, inspired from above, writ nothing but truth."
And, to the same effect, in his Second Reply to Stillingfleet, he writes :—" My lord, I read the revelation of the
holy scripture with a full assurance that all it delivers is
true."   The word " infallible " is applied, without any
misgiving or qualification, to the contents of Scripture,
though he assumes to each individual believer full liberty
of interpretation.   During his residence in Holland, as we
have already seen, he appears to have entertained some
doubts on this subject, but, at a later period, those doubts
appear to have been finally laid.

Notwithstanding, however, the sincerity and simplicity
of Locke's religious faith, the doctrines which he maintained must have represented but a very attenuated
Christianity to the partisans of the two great religious
parties which were at that time nominally the strongest in
England.   A Christianity which did not recognize the
hereditary taint of original sin, and which passed over the
mystery of the Atonement in silence, must have been as
distasteful to one party as a Christianity which ignored

Church authority and the exclusive privileges of the apostolical succession must have been to the other.   And to the zealots of both parties alike, a statement of doctrine which was silent on the mystery of the Trinity, or rather which seemed to imply that the Son, though miraculously conceived, was not co-equal or co-eternal with the Father, and which, by implication, appeared to suggest that, though the righteous would be endowed with immortality, the torments of the wicked would have an end, might well seem not to deserve the name of Christianity at all.   We need feel no wonder, then, that the appearance of Locke's work was followed by a bitter theological controversy which lasted during the rest of his life, and beyond it. Of these attacks upon him, and his *Vindications,* I have spoken in a previous chapter.

Whether Locke's presentation of Christianity is really more "reasonable" than the ancient and venerable creeds which it attempted to replace, is a question which might be debated now with fully as much vigour as in his own day.   On the one hand, it might be maintained that a religion which has no mysteries, which has been pared down to the requirements of human reason, has ceased to be a religion altogether.   That which is behind the veil can only be partially revealed in our present condition and to our present faculties.   Now we know, and can know, only in part.   On the other hand, it might be said that the "reason" is quite as much offended by the doctrines which Locke retained as by those which he rejected. It is necessary, however, to recollect, in estimating his position, that the theological difficulties of his age were moral and metaphysical rather than scientific and critical. The moral consciousness of many reflecting men was shocked by doctrines like those of original sin, predestina-

M

tion, the atonement, and everlasting punishment. Nor
could they reconcile to their reason the seeming contradictions of the doctrine of a Triune God. But the study
of nature had not advanced sufficiently far, or been sufficiently widely spread, to make the idea of supernatural
intervention in the ordinary course of affairs, such as is
constantly presented to us in the Biblical history, any
serious or general stumbling-block. Much less had the
criticism of the Sacred Text, or the comparison of it with
the sacred books of other religions, become sufficiently
common, or been carried out with sufficient rigour, to
disturb, to any great extent, the received opinion that the
Bible was literally, or, at least, substantially, the Word of
God. Hence, the *via media* on which Locke took his
stand, though it might have been impossible to a philosopher of the next generation, seemed reasonable and natural
enough to speculative men among his contemporaries.
And for him it had at least this advantage, that it enabled
him honestly to reconcile the conclusions of his philosophy
with the singular piety and devoutness of his disposition.
Had his religious doubts proceeded further than they did,
there would probably have ensued a mental struggle
which, besides causing him much personal unhappiness,
might have deprived posterity of the more important of
his works.

Of *The Letters on Toleration*, though deeply interesting to the generation in which they were written, a
very brief account will here suffice. Their main thesis
is, that the jurisdiction of the civil magistrate does
not extend to the regulation of religious worship or to
controlling the expression of religious beliefs, except
so far as that worship or those beliefs may interfere

with the ends of civil government. The respective
provinces of a commonwealth and a church are strictly
defined, and are shown to be perfectly distinct. "The
boundaries on both sides are fixed and immovable. He
jumbles heaven and earth together, the things most
remote and opposite, who mixes these societies, which
are in their orginal, end, business, and in everything,
perfectly distinct and infinitely different from each
other." But it may be asked, are there no speculative
opinions, no tenets, actual or possible, of any religious
community which should be restrained by the Civil Magistrate? The answer is, yes,—

"First, No opinions contrary to human society, or to those
moral rules which are necessary to the preservation of civil
society, are to be tolerated by the magistrate."

Secondly, after speaking of those who maintain such
positions as that "faith is not to be kept with heretics,"
that "kings excommunicated forfeit their crowns and
kingdoms," that "dominion is founded in grace," he proceeds :

"These, therefore, and the like, who attribute unto the faithful,
religious, and orthodox, that is, in plain terms, unto themselves,
any peculiar privilege or power above other mortals in civil con-
cernments, or who, upon pretence of religion, do challenge any
manner of authority over such as are not associated with them
in their ecclesiastical communion : I say these have no right to be
tolerated by the magistrate, as neither those that will not own and
teach the duty of tolerating all men in matters of mere religion.
For what do all these and the like doctrines signify, but that
they may, and are ready upon any occasion to seize the government, and possess themselves of the estates and fortunes of their
fellow-subjects, and that they only ask leave to be tolerated by
the magistrates so long until they find themselves strong enough
to effect it?"

"Thirdly, That church can have no right to be tolerated by the magistrate, which is constituted upon such a bottom that all those who enter upon it do thereby ipso facto deliver themselves up to the protection and service of another prince. For by this means the magistrate would give way to the settling of a foreign jurisdiction in his own country, and suffer his own people to be listed, as it were, for soldiers against his own government."

"Lastly, Those are not at all to be tolerated who deny the being of God. Promises, covenants, and oaths, which are the bonds of human society, can have no hold upon an atheist. The taking away of God, though but even in thought, dissolves all."

The practical result of Locke's exceptions, at the time at which he wrote, would have been to exclude from toleration Roman Catholics, Atheists, and perhaps certain sects of Antinomians. Roman Catholics, however, would not have been excluded on the ground of their belief in Transubstantiation, as was actually the case, but because of those tenets which, in Locke's judgment, made them bad or impossible subjects.

Locke was not, by any means, the first of English writers who had advocated a wide toleration in religion. Bacon, in his remarkable *Essay on Unity in Religion*, had laid down, in passing, a position which is almost identical with that developed at length in the *Letters on Toleration*. During the Civil Wars, the Independents, as a body, had been led on by their theories of Church Government and of individual inspiration to maintain, on principle, and accord, in practice, a large, measure of religious toleration. Amongst divines of the Church of England, Hales of Eton, Chillingworth, and Jeremy Taylor, had honourably distinguished themselves above the mass of their brethren by expressly advocating, or unmistakably suggesting, the same humane doctrines.

The practical conclusions at which Taylor arrives in his
noble work on the *Liberty of Prophesying* bear a close
resemblance to those of Locke's *Letters on Toleration*,
while the theoretical considerations on which he mainly
founds them, namely, the difficulty of discovering religious truth and the small number of theological propositions of which we can entertain anything like certainty,
might be regarded as anticipating, to no small extent,
some of the views expressed in the *Reasonableness of
Christianity*. Locke's attention had been turned to these
questions at an early period of his life by the religious
dissensions which accompanied the Civil Wars, and,
during the years immediately preceding the publication
of the first *Letter on Toleration*, his interest in them
must have been sustained not only by the events which
were then happening in England but by the common
topics of conversation amongst his Arminian or Remonstrant friends in Holland. The peculiarities of their
position and the tendencies of their doctrines had, at an
early date, forced on the Dutch Remonstrants, just as on
the English Independents, the necessity of claiming and
defending a wide toleration. What, perhaps, mainly distinguishes Locke's pamphlets is their thorough outspokenness, the political rather than the theological character
of the argument, and the fact that they are expressly
dedicated to the subject of Toleration, instead of treating
of it incidentally.

The sharp line of demarcation which Locke draws
between the respective provinces of civil and religious
communities seems to lead logically to the inexpediency
of maintaining a state establishment of religion. The
independence which he claims for all religious societies
would be inconsistent with the control which the State

always has exercised, and always must exercise, in the
affairs of any spiritual body on which it confers special
privileges. This conclusion, we can hardly doubt, he
would have readily accepted. As far back as 1669, he
had objected to one of the articles in the "Fundamental
Constitutions of Carolina," providing for the establishment and endowment of the Church of England in that
colony. Even at the present day, men who adopt the
most liberal and tolerant opinions on religious questions
are divided as to the expediency or inexpediency of
recognizing a State-Church, but those who embrace the
latter alternative may, perhaps, fairly claim Locke as
having been on their side.

The system contained in the *Reasonableness of
Christianity* had been constructed solely on an examination of the Gospels and the Acts of the Apostles. In
addition to the difficulties of interpretation attaching to
the Epistles, Locke had urged that "they were writ to
them who were in the faith and true Christians already,
and so could not be designed to teach them the fundamental articles and points necessary to salvation." But
to one who accepted the divine inspiration and infallibility of all parts of Scripture, it was essential to establish
the consistency and coherence of the whole. Accordingly,
in the later years of his life, Locke set himself the task
of explaining the Epistles. This work seems to have
been undertaken more for his own satisfaction and that
of Lady Masham and his more immediate friends, than
with any distinct design of publication. Nor did his
commentaries see the light till after his death.

The commentatorial work accomplished by Locke con-
sists of paraphrases and notes on the Epistles to the

Galatians, Corinthians, Romans, and Ephesians, together with *An Essay for the understanding of St. Paul's Epistles by consulting St. Paul himself.*

It is needless to remark that these commentaries are distinguished by sound, clear sense, and by a manifest spirit of candour and fairness. They are often quoted with approbation by commentators of the last century. But in the present more advanced state of grammatical and historical criticism, they are likely to remain, as they now are, the least consulted of all his works.

The method, object, and drift of all Locke's theological writings is the same. Regardless of ecclesiastical tradition, but assuming the infallibility of the Scriptures, he attempts to arrive at the true and essential import of God's Revelation to man. His theoretical conclusion is that the articles of saving faith are few and simple, and the practical application of that conclusion is that, not only within the ample fold of Christianity, but even without it, all men, whose conduct is consistent with the maintenance of civil society, should be the objects of our good-will and charity.

CHAPTER X.

LOCKE'S tractate on Education, though some of the maxims
are reiterated with needless prolixity, abounds in shrewd-
ness and common-sense. Taking as the object of education the production of "a sound mind in a sound body,"
he begins with the "case," the "clay-cottage," and considers first the health of the body. Of the diet prescribed,
dry bread and small beer form a large proportion. Locke
is a great believer in the virtues of cold water. Coddling,
in all its forms, was to be repressed with a strong hand.
My young master was to be much in the open air, he was
to play in the wind and the sun without a hat, his clothes
were not to be too warm, and his bed was to be hard and
made in different fashions, that he might not in after-life
feel every little change, when there was no maid " to lay
all things in print, and tuck him in warm."

In the cultivation of the mind, far more importance is
attached to the formation of virtuous habits and even of
those social qualities which go by the name of "good
breeding" than to the mere inculcation of knowledge. "I
place Virtue as the first and most necessary of those en-
dowments that belong to a Man or a Gentleman; as absolutely requisite to make him valued and beloved by others,

acceptable or tolerable to himself." Wisdom, that is to say, "a man's managing his business ably, and with foresight, in this world," comes next in order. In the third place is Good Breeding, the breaches of which may be all avoided by "observing this one rule, Not to think meanly of ourselves, and not to think meanly of others." Learning, though "this may seem strange in the mouth of a bookish man," he puts last. "When I consider what ado is made about a little Latin and Greek, how many years are spent in it, and what a noise and business it makes to no purpose, I can hardly forbear thinking that the parents of children still live in fear of the Schoolmaster's Rod." "Seek out some body that may know how discreetly to frame your child's manners : place him in hands where you may, as much as possible, secure his innocence, cherish and nurse up the good, and gently correct and weed out any bad inclinations, and settle in him good habits. This is the main point, and, this being provided for, Learning may be had into the bargain, and that, as I think" (a very common delusion among the educational reformers of Locke's time), "at a very easy rate, by methods that may be thought on."

These being Locke's ideas as to the relative value of the objects to be aimed at in education, we need feel little surprise at the disfavour with which he viewed the system of the English Public Schools.

"Till you can find a School, wherein it is possible for the Master to look after the manners of his scholars, and can show as great efforts of his care of forming their minds to virtue and their carriage to good breeding as of forming their tongues to the learned languages, you must confess that you have a strange value for words when, preferring the languages of the ancient Greeks and Romans to that which made 'em such brave

men, you think it worth while to hazard your son's innocence and
virtue for a little Greek and Latin. How any one's being put
into a mixed herd of unruly boys, and there learning to wrangle
at Trap or rook at Span-Farthing fits him for civil conversation
or business, I do not see. And what qualities are ordinarily to
be got from such a troop of Play-fellows as Schools usually
assemble together from parents of all kinds, that a father should
so much covet, is hard to divine. I am sure he who is able to
be at the charge of a Tutor at home may there give his son a
more genteel carriage, more manly thoughts, and a sense of
what is worthy and becoming, with a greater proficiency in
Learning into the bargain, and ripen him up sooner into a man,
than any at School can do."

The battle of private and public education has been
waged more or less fiercely ever since Locke's time, as it
was waged long before, and, although it has now been
generally decided in favour of the Schools, many of his
arguments have even yet not lost their force.

Not only in the interest of morality, character, and
manners did Locke disapprove the Public School system
of his day. He also thought it essentially defective in its
subjects and modes of instruction. The subjects taught
were almost exclusively the Latin and Greek languages,
though at Locke's own school of Westminster the upper
forms were also initiated into Hebrew and Arabic. This
linguistic training, though of course it included translations from the classical authors, was to a large extent
carried on by means of verse-making, theme-making, repetition, and grammar lessons. Against all these modes of
teaching Locke is peculiarly severe. Grammar indeed he
would have taught, but not till the pupil is sufficiently
conversant with the language to be able to speak it with
tolerable fluency. Its proper place is as an introduction
to Rhetoric. " I know not why any one should waste his

time and beat his head about the Latin Grammar, who does not intend to be a critic, or make speeches and write despatches in it. . . . If his use of it be only to understand some books writ in it, without a critical knowledge of the tongue itself, reading alone will attain this end, without charging the mind with the multiplied rules and intricacies of Grammar." But without a knowledge of some rules of grammar, which need not, however, be taught in an abstract and separate form, but may be learnt gradually in the course of reading, writing, and speaking, how would it be possible to attain to any precise understanding of the authors read? The fault of the old system, which even still lingers on in school instruction, consisted not so much in teaching grammatical rules, as in teaching them apart from the writings which exemplify them, and which alone can render them intelligible or interesting to a beginner.

The practice of filling up a large part of a boy's time with making Latin themes and verses meets with still more scathing censure than that of initiating him into the learned languages by means of abstract rules of grammar, and we may well imagine the cordial assent with which many of Locke's readers, smarting under a sense of the time they had in this way lost at school, would receive his criticisms.

"For do but consider what it is in making a Theme that a young lad is employed about; it is to make a speech on some Latin saying, as *Omnia vincit amor*, or *Non licet in bello bis peccare*, &c. And here the poor lad, who wants knowledge of those things he is to speak of, which is to be had only from time and observation, must set his invention on the rack to say something where he knows nothing; which is a sort of Egyptian tyranny to bid them make bricks who have not yet any of the materials. . . . . In the next place consider the

Language that their Themes are made in. 'Tis Latin, a language foreign in their country, and long since dead everywhere: a language which your son, 'tis a thousand to one, shall never have an occasion once to make a speech in as long as he lives after he comes to be a man; and a language wherein the manner of expressing one's self is so far different from ours that to be perfect in that would very little improve the purity and facility of his English style."

"If these may be any reasons against children's making Latin Themes at school, I have much more to say, and of more weight, against their making verses; verses of any sort. For if he has no genius to poetry, 'tis the most unreasonable thing in the world to torment a child and waste his time about that which can never succeed; and if he have a poetic vein, 'tis to me the strangest thing in the world that the father should desire or suffer it to be cherished or improved. Methinks the parents should labour to have it stifled and suppressed as much as may be; and I know not what reason a father can have to wish his son a poet, who does not desire to have him bid defiance to all other callings and business. Which is not yet the worst of the case; for if he proves a successful rhymer, and get once the reputation of a Wit, I desire it may be considered what company and places he is likely to spend his time in, nay, and estate too. For it is very seldom seen that any one discovers mines of gold or silver in Parnassus. 'Tis a pleasant air, but a barren soil; and there are very few instances of those who have added to their patrimony by anything they have reaped from thence. Poetry and Gaming, which usually go together, are alike in this too, that they seldom bring any advantage but to those who have nothing else to live on."

Repetition, as it is called, or "learning by heart great parcels of the authors which are taught," is unreservedly condemned as being of "no use at all, unless it be to baulk young lads in the way to learning languages, which, in my opinion, should be made as easy and pleasant as may be." "Languages are to be learned only by reading

and talking, and not by scraps of authors got by heart ;
which when a man's head is stuffed with, he has got the
just furniture of a pedant, than which there is nothing
less becoming a gentleman." This unqualified condemna-
tion of the practice of committing to memory the choicer
pieces of classical authors, whether in the ancient or
modern languages, would hardly be adopted by the educational reformers of our own day. To tax the memory of
a child or a boy with long strings of words, ill understood
or not understood at all, is about as cruel and senseless a
practice as can well be conceived. It is one of the strange
devices, invented by perverse pedagogues and tolerated
by ignorant parents, through which literature and all that
is connected with books has been made so repulsive to
many generations of young Englishmen. But, if the
tastes and interests of the pupil are skilfully consulted,
and the understanding is called into action as well as the
memory, a store of well-selected passages learnt by rote
will not only do much to familiarize him with the genius
of the language, but will also supply constant solace
and occupation in those moments of depression and
vacuity which are only too sure to occur in every man's
life.

Locke, like Milton (see Milton's Pamphlet on Education
addressed to Master Samuel Hartlib, and cp. Pattison's
Life of Milton, published in this series, pp. 45—49),
had embraced the new gospel of education according to
Comenius, and supposed that, by new methods, not only
might the road to knowledge be rendered very short and
easy, but almost all the subjects worth learning might be
taught in the few years spent at School and College. The
whole of Milton's " complete and generous education "
was to be "done between twelve and one-and-twenty."

And similarly Locke thinks that "at the same time that a child is learning French and Latin, he may also be entered in Arithmetic, Geography, Chronology, History, and Geometry too. For if these be taught him in French or Latin, when he begins once to understand either of these tongues, he will get a knowledge in these sciences and the language to boot." To these subjects are afterwards added Astronomy, Ethics, Civil and Common Law, Natural Philosophy, and almost all the then known branches of human knowledge, though, curiously enough, Greek is omitted as not being, like Latin and French, essential to the education of a gentleman, and being, moreover, easy of acquisition, "if he has a mind to carry his studies farther," in after-life. Concurrently with these intellectual pursuits, the model young gentleman is to graduate in dancing, fencing, wrestling, riding, besides (and on this addition to his accomplishments the utmost stress is laid) "learning a trade, a manual trade, nay, two or three, but one more particularly." And all this programme apparently was to be filled up before the age of one-and-twenty, for at that time Locke assumes that, notwithstanding all reasons and remonstrances to the contrary, my young master's parents will insist on marrying him, and "the young gentleman being got within view of matrimony, 'tis time to leave him to his mistress." This idea of an education embracing the whole field of human knowledge and accomplishments is a vision so attractive, that it would be strange indeed if it did not from time to time present itself to the enthusiast and the reformer. But, wherever the experiment has been tried on boys or youths of average strength and ability, the vision has invariably been dissipated. And, as the circle of human knowledge is constantly widening, whereas the capacity to learn remains much the same from generation to generation, the failure is inevitable.

Any account of Locke's views on Education, however meagre, would be very imperfect, if it neglected to notice the motives to obedience and proficiency which he proposed to substitute for what was then too often the one and only motive on which the Schoolmaster relied, fear of the rod. Corporal chastisement should be reserved, he thought, for the offence of wilful and obstinate disobedience. In all other cases, appeal should be made to the pupil's natural desire of employment and knowledge, to example acting through his propensity to imitation, to reasoning, to the sense of shame and the love of commendation and reputation. Many of Locke's suggestions for bringing these motives effectually to bear are very ingenious, and the whole of this part of the discussion is as creditable to his humanity as to his knowledge of human nature.

There is a large literature on the theory of education from the Book of Proverbs and the *Republic* of Plato downwards. It is no part of my task even to mention the principal writers in this field. But, besides some of the works of Comenius, the Essay of Montaigne *De l'institution des enfants,* and the tractate of Milton already referred to, we may almost take for granted that Locke had read the *Schoolmaster* of Roger Ascham. This author, who was instructor to Queen Elizabeth, is already sufficiently independent of scholastic traditions, to think that "children are sooner allured by love, than driven by beating, to attain good learning," and to suggest that "there is no such whetstone to sharpen a good wit, and encourage a will to learning, as is praise." He protests almost as strongly as Locke against the senseless mode, then and long afterwards prevalent, of teaching grammar merely by means of abstract rules, and proposes, as in part substitute, the method of double translation, that is of translating from the foreign or dead language into English, and then back again. Of the many works on education subsequent to Locke's, the most famous is, undoubtedly, the *Emile* of Rousseau. On Rousseau's theories there can be no question that Locke, mediately or immediately, exercised considerable influence, though the range of speculation covered in the *Emile* far exceeds that of the *Thoughts concerning Education.* Of the points common to the two writers, I may specify the extension of the term "education" to the regulations of the nursery, the substitution of an appeal to the tender and the social affections for the harsh discipline mostly in vogue among our ancestors, the stress laid on the importance of example and habituation in place of the mere inculcation of rules, and, as a point of detail, the desirableness of learning one or more manual trades. One circumstance, however, as Mr. Morley has pointed out, distinguishes the *Emile* from all the works on education which preceded it. Its scope is not confined to the children of well-to-do people, and hence its object is to produce, not the scholar and the gentleman, but the man. The democratic extension thus given to educational theories has since borne fruit in many schemes designed for general applicability, or, specifically, for the education of the poor, such as those of Basedow, Pestalozzi, and, among our own countrymen, Dr. Bell.

In connexion with the *Thoughts on Education*, it may be convenient to notice the short treatise on the *Conduct of the Understanding.* It is true that it was designed as an additional chapter to the *Essay*, but the main theme of which it treats is connected rather with the work of self-education than with the analysis of knowledge, or the classification of the faculties. This admirable little volume, which may be read through in three or four hours, appears to have been intended by Locke as at least a partial substitute for the ordinary logic. As in matters of conduct, so in the things of the intellect, he thought little of rules. It was only by practice and habituation that men could become either virtuous or wise. But, though it is perfectly true that rules are of little use without practice, it is not easy to see how habit can be successfully initiated or fostered without the assistance of rules; and inadequate as were the rules of the old scholastic logic to remedy the "natural defects in the understanding," they required rather to be supplemented than replaced. The views of Bacon on this subject, much as they have been misunderstood, are juster than those of Locke.

Right reasoning, Locke thought (and this is nearly the whole truth, though not altogether so), is to be gained from studying good models of it. In the *Thoughts on Education*, he says, "If you would have your son reason well, let him read Chillingworth." In this treatise, with the same view he commends the study of Mathematics, "not that I think it necessary that all men should be deep mathematicians, but that, having got the way of reasoning which that study necessarily brings the mind to, they might be able to transfer it to other parts of knowledge, as they shall have occasion." The great difference to be observed in demonstrative and in probable reasoning is that, in the former one train of reasoning, " bringing the mind to the source on which it bottoms,"

N

is sufficient, whereas "in probabilities it is not enough to trace one argument to its source, and observe its strength and weakness, but all the arguments, after having been so examined on both sides, must be laid in balance one against another, and, upon the whole, the understanding determine its assent."

The great defect of this tractate (but its brevity makes the defect of less importance) is its singular want of method. In fact, it appears never to have undergone revision. The author seems to throw together his remarks and precepts without any attempt at order, and he never misses any opportunity of repeating his attacks on what he evidently regarded as being, in his own time, the main hindrances to the acquisition of a sound understanding,—prejudice and pedantry. But in justness of observation, incisiveness of language, and profound acquaintance with the workings of the human mind, there are many passages which will bear comparison with anything he has written. Specially worthy of notice is the homely and forcible character of many of his expressions, as when he speaks of a "large, sound, roundabout sense," of "men without any industry or acquisition of their own, inheriting local truths," of great readers "making their understanding only the warehouse of other men's lumber," of the ruling passion entering the mind, like "the sheriff of the place, with all the posse, as if it had a legal right to be alone considered there."

Except for the inveterate and growing custom of confining works employed in education to such as can be easily lectured on and easily examined in, it is difficult to understand why this "student's guide," so brief and abounding in such valuable cautions and suggestions, should have so nearly fallen into desuetude.

CHAPTER XI.

LOCKE's two *Treatises of Government* (published in 1690) carry us back into the region of worn-out controversies. The troublous times which intervened between the outbreak of the Civil War and the Revolution of 1688, including some years on either side, naturally called forth a large amount of controversy and controversial literature on the rights of kings and subjects, on the origin of government, on the point at which, if any, rebellion is justifiable, and other kindred topics. Not only did the press teem with pamphlets on these subjects, but, for three-quarters of a century, they were constantly being discussed and re-discussed with a dreary monotony in parliament, in the pulpits, in the courts of law, and in the intercourse of private society. It is no part of my plan to give any account of these disputes, except so far as they bear immediately on the publication of Locke's treatises. It is enough, therefore, to state that the despotic and absolutist side in the controversy had been, or was supposed to have been, considerably re-inforced by the appearance in 1680 of a posthumous work, which had been circulated only in manuscript during its author's life time, entitled *Patriarcha or the Natural Power of Kings*, by Sir Robert Filmer. This curious book (a more correct

edition of which was published by Edmund Bohun in
1685) grounds the rights of kings on the patriarchal
authority of Adam and his successors. Adam had received
directly from God (such was the theory) absolute dominion over Eve and all his children and their posterity,
to the most remote generations. This dominion, which
rested on two independent grounds, paternity and right
of property, was transmitted by Adam to his heirs, and is
at once the justification of the various sovereignties now
exercised by kings over their subjects, and a reason against
any limitation of their authority or any questioning of
their titles. By what ingenious contrivances the two
links of the chain, Adam and the several monarchs now
actually reigning on the earth, are brought together, those
curious in such speculations may find by duly consulting
the pages of Sir Robert Filmer's work.

Such a tissue of contradictions, assumptions, and absurdities as is presented by this book (which, however, contains one grain of truth, namely, that all political power
has, historically, its ultimate origin in the dominion exercised by the head of the family or tribe) might have been
left, one would think, without any serious answer. But
we must recollect that, at that time, theological arguments
were introduced into all the provinces of thought, and that
any reason, which by any supposition could be connected
with the authority of Scripture, was certain to exercise
considerable influence over a vast number of minds. Any
way, the book was celebrated and influential enough to
merit, in Locke's judgment, a detailed answer. This answer was given in due form, step by step, in the former
of Locke's two *Treatises*, which appears to have been
written between 1680 and 1685, as the Edition of the
Patriarcha quoted is invariably that of 1680. I do not

propose to follow him through his various arguments and criticisms, many of which, as will readily be supposed, are acute and sagacious enough. Most modern readers will be of opinion that one of his questions might alone have sufficed to spare him any further concern, namely, Where is Adam's heir now to be found? If he could be shown, and his title indubitably proved, the subsequent question of his rights and prerogatives might then, perhaps, be profitably discussed.

Of incomparably more importance and interest than the former treatise, is the latter, in which Locke sets forth his own theory concerning "the true original, extent, and end of Civil Government." Mr. Fox Bourne is probably correct in referring the date of the composition of this treatise to the time immediately preceding and concurrent with the English Revolution, that is to say, to the closing period of Locke's stay in Holland. The work, especially in the later chapters, bears the marks of passion, as if written in the midst of a great political struggle, and, in the Preface to the two *Treatises*, it is distinctly stated to be the author's object "to establish the throne of our great restorer, our present King William, and to justify to the world the people of England, whose love of their just and natural rights saved the nation when it was on the very brink of slavery and ruin."

The theories advanced by Locke on the origin and nature of civil society have much in common with those of Puffendorf and Hooker, the latter of whom is constantly quoted in the foot-notes. After some preliminary speculations on the "state of nature," he determines that Political Society originates solely in the individual consents of those who constitute it. This consent, however, may be signified either expressly or tacitly, and the tacit consent

" reaches as far as the very being of any one within the territories of that government."

Though no man need enter a political society against his will, yet when, by consent given either expressly or tacitly, he has entered it, he must submit to the form of government established by the majority. There is, however, one form of government which it is not competent even to the majority to establish, and that is Absolute Monarchy, this being " inconsistent with civil society, and so being no form of government at all." Locke ridicules the idea that men would ever voluntarily have erected over themselves such an authority, " as if, when men quitting the state of nature entered into society, they agreed that all of them but one should be under the restraint of laws, but that he should still retain all the liberty of the state of nature, increased with power and made licentious by impunity. This is to think that men are so foolish, that they take care to avoid what mischiefs may be done them by pole-cats or foxes, but are content, nay, think it safety, to be devoured by lions." In these and some of the following strictures, he seems to have in view not only the ruder theories of Filmer and the absolutist divines, but also the more philosophical system of Hobbes.

But, supposing a government other than an Absolute Monarchy to have been established, are there any acts or omissions by which it can forfeit the allegiance of its subjects? To answer this question, we must look to the ends of political society and government. Now the great and chief end which men propose to themselves, when they unite into commonwealths, is " the mutual preservation of their lives, liberties, and estates, which I call by the general name, property." A government, therefore, which neglects to secure this end, and still more a government which itself invades the rights of its subjects, is guilty of a breach of trust, and consequently may be lawfully set aside, whenever an opportunity occurs. Hence, the community itself must always be regarded as the supreme authority, in abeyance indeed while its fiduciary properly and faithfully executes the powers entrusted to him, but ever ready to intervene, when he misuses or betrays the trust reposed in him.

On such a theory, it may be objected, of the relations of the people to the government, what is to prevent incessant disturbance and repeated revolutions? Locke relies on the inertia of mankind. Moreover, as he says, with considerable truth, in a previous passage, whatever theories may be propounded, or whatever traditions may have been handed down, as to the origin, nature, and extent of government, a people, which knows itself to be rendered miserable by the faults of its rulers and which sees any chance of bettering its condition, will not be deterred from attempting to throw off a yoke which has become intolerable. " When the people are made miserable, and find themselves exposed to the ill-usage of arbitrary power, cry up their governors, as much as you will, for sons of Jupiter ; let them be sacred and divine, descended or authorized from heaven ; give them out for whom or what you please, the same will happen. The people generally ill-treated, and contrary to right, will be ready upon any occasion to ease themselves of a burden that sits heavy upon them."

But, though there is much truth in this last remark, there can be little question that absolutist theories of government, especially when clothed with a religious sanction which appeals to the beliefs of the people at large, have much influence in protecting the person of an absolute ruler, as well as in ensuring the execution of his orders; while, on the other hand, theories like those of Locke have a tendency to encourage criticism and to weaken many of the motives which have usually prevented men from offering resistance to the established government. The practical consequences of Locke's theories, as reproduced and improved on by later writers, would probably be found, if we could trace them, to be represented, in no inconsiderable degree, in the French and American revolutions which occurred about a century after the publication of the Treatises. Nor have his speculations been without their share, probably, in determining much of the political history and still more of the political sentiment of our own country. To maintain that kings have a divine right to misgovern their subjects, or to deny that the people are, in the last resort, the supreme arbiters of the fate of their rulers, are paradoxes which, to Englishmen of our generation, would appear not so much dangerous as foolish. This altered state of sentiment and the good fruit it has borne in the improved relations between the Legislature and the People, the Crown and the Parliament, may, without undue partiality, be ascribed, at least in some measure, to the generous spirit of liberty which warms our author's pages, and to the Whig tradition which so long cherished his doctrines, till at last they became the common heritage of the English people.

Admirable, however, as, in most respects, are the parts of Locke's treatise which discuss the present relations of governors and governed, his conception of the remote origin of political society is radically false. "The first framers of the government," "the original frame of the government" (ch. xiii.) have never had any existence except in the minds of jurists and publicists. In the primitive stages of human development, governments, like languages, are not made; they grow. The observation of primitive communities still existing, combined with the more intelligent study of ancient history, has led recent writers to adopt a wholly different view of the *origin* of government (the question of the respective *rights* of governors and governed is not affected) from that which prevailed in the times of Hobbes, Locke, and Rousseau. The family or the tribe (according to different theories) is the original unit of society. Government, therefore, of some kind or other must always have existed, and the "state of nature" is a mere fiction. In course of time, the family or the tribe, by a natural process of development, would, in many cases, become greatly enlarged or combine with other units like itself. Out of this growth or aggregation would arise, in most cases gradually and insensibly, the nation or state as known to later history. The constitution, the "frame of government," has generally passed through stages similar to those passed through by the state or nation. A body of custom must gradually have grown up even in the most primitive societies. The "customs" would be interpreted and so administered by the house-father or head of the tribe. But, as the family or tribe changed its abode, or had to carry on its existence under different circumstances, or became enlarged, or combined with other families or tribes, the customs would necessarily be modified, often insensibly and unconsciously. Moreover, the house-father or head of the tribe might be compelled or might find it expedient to act in concert with others, either as equals or subordinates, in interpreting the customs, in taking measures of defence, in directing military operations, or in providing for the various exigencies of the common

life. Here there is no formal assent of the governed to
the acts of the governors, in our sense of those terms,
though, undoubtedly, the whole family or tribe, or its
stronger members, might on rare occasions substitute one
head for another ; no passage from the " state of nature "
to political society ; no definitely constituted "frame of
government." At a further stage, no doubt, political
constitutions were discussed and framed, but this stage
was long posterior to the period in the progress of society
at which men are supposed to have quitted the state of
nature, selected their form of government, and entered
into an express contract with one another to obey and
maintain it. The fault of Locke, like that of the other
political speculators of the seventeenth and eighteenth centuries, consisted in assuming that primitive man was
impelled by the same motives, and acted in the same manner and with the same deliberate design, as the men of
his own generation. As in morals and psychology, so
in politics, the historical and comparative methods,
so familiar to recent investigators, were as yet hardly
known.

I ought not to dismiss this book, without noticing
Locke's remarks on the necessity of Parliamentary Reform. "To what gross absurdities the following of custom, when reason has left it, may lead, we may be satisfied
when we see the bare name of a town, of which there
remains not so much as the ruins, where scarce so much
housing as a sheepcote or more inhabitants than a shep-
herd is to be found, sends as many representatives to the
grand assembly of law-makers as a whole county numerous
in people and powerful in riches."

The writings of Locke on Trade and Finance are

chiefly interesting to us on account of the place which
they occupy in the History of Political Economy. They
consist of three tracts, the occasions and consequences of
which have already been described. The main positions
which he endeavours to establish are three. First, interest,
or the price of the hire of money, cannot, ordinarily
speaking, be regulated by law, and, if it could so be regulated, its reduction below the natural or market rate
would be injurious to the interests of the public. Secondly,
as silver and gold are commodities not differing intrin-
sically in their nature from other commodities, it is
impossible by arbitrary acts of the Government to raise
the value of silver and gold coins. You may indeed
enjoin by Act of Parliament that sixpence shall henceforth
be called a shilling, but, all the same, it will only con-
tinue to purchase sixpenny-worth of goods. You will
soon find that the new shilling is only as effective in the
market as the old sixpence, and hence, if the Government
has taken the difference, it has simply robbed its subjects
to that amount. The third position, which he only
maintains incidentally in discussing the other two, is that
the commercial prosperity of a country is to be measured
by the excess of its exports over its imports, or, as the
phrase then went, by the balance of trade. The two
former of these propositions are simple, but long-disputed,
economical truths. The latter is an obstinate and specious
economical fallacy.

To understand Locke's contention on the first point, it
must be borne in mind that in his time, and down even to
the middle of the present reign, the maximum rate of interest allowable in all ordinary transactions was fixed by law.
By the statute 12 Car. II. (passed in 1660) it had been
reduced from eight to six per cent. Sir Josiah Child, whose

Observations concerning Trade had been reprinted in 1690,
and who probably represented a very large amount of
mercantile opinion, advocated its further reduction to
four per cent. He maintained, quoting the example of
Holland, that low interest is the cause of national wealth,
and that, consequently, to lower the legal rate of interest
would be to take a speedy and simple method of making
the country richer. Against this proposal Locke argued
that the example of Holland was entirely beside the question ; that the low rate of interest in that country was owing
to the abundance of ready money which it had formerly
enjoyed, and not to any legal restrictions ; nay, in the
States there was no law limiting the rate of interest at all,
every one being free to hire out his money for anything
he could get for it, and the courts enforcing the bargain.
But, further, suppose the proposed law to be enacted ;
what would be the consequences ? It would be certain to
be evaded, while, at the same time, it would hamper
trade, by increasing the difficulty of borrowing and
lending. Rather than lend at a low rate of interest,
many men would hoard, and, consequently, much of the
money, which would otherwise find its way into trade,
would be intercepted, and the commerce of the country
be proportionately lessened. Excellent as most of these
arguments are, Locke unfortunately stopped short of the
legitimate conclusion to be drawn from them. He did
not propose, as he should have done, to sweep away the
usury laws altogether, but simply to maintain the existing
law fixing the maximum of interest at six per cent. Sir
Dudley North, in his admirable pamphlet *Discourses on
Trade*, published in 1691, just before the publication of
the *Considerations*, but too late, perhaps, to have been
seen by Locke, takes a much more consistent view as to

the expediency of legal restrictions on the rate of interest. " As touching interest of money, he is clear that it should be left freely to the market, and not be restrained by law." Notwithstanding the opposition of men like North and Locke, to whom may be added an earlier writer, Sir William Petty, the arguments of Child partially triumphed in the next reign. By the 12th of Anne, the legal rate of interest was reduced to five per cent., and so continued till the Act of 1854, repealing, with regard to all future transactions, the existing Usury Laws. There can be little doubt that public opinion had been prepared for this measure mainly through the publication of Bentham's powerful *Defence of Usury*, the telling arguments of which had gradually impressed themselves on the minds of statesmen and economists. Adam Smith, on the other hand, had stopped just where Locke did. " The legal rate of interest, though it ought to be somewhat above, ought not to be much above the lowest market rate." That the rate of interest, whatever it may be, should be fixed by law, he appears to take for granted. Indeed, he seems to write more confidently on this point than Locke had done, and, in this particular at least, appears to be of opinion that the legislator can look after the private interests of individuals better than they can look after their own. Happily, as Bentham points out, the refutation of this paradox was to be found in the general drift and spirit of his work.

On the second question, " raising the value of money," Locke's views are much clearer and more consistent than on the first. It would be impossible to state more explicitly than he has done the sound economical dictum that gold and silver are simply commodities, not differing essen-

tially from other commodities, and that the government
stamp upon them, whereby they become coin, cannot
materially raise their value. As most of my readers are,
aware, it has been a favourite device, time out of mind, of
unprincipled and impecunious governments to raise the
denomination of the coin, or to put a smaller quantity of
the precious metals in coins retaining the old denomination, with the view of recruiting an impoverished exchequer. There have, doubtless, been financiers unintelligent
enough to suppose that this expedient might enrich the
government, while it did no harm to the people. But it
requires only a slight amount of reflection to see that all
creditors are defrauded exactly in the same proportion as
that in which the coin is debased. One lucid passage
from Locke's answer to Lowndes may suffice to show the
forcible manner in which he presents this truth.

"Raising of coin is but a specious word to deceive the un-
wary. It only gives the usual denomination of a greater quantity of silver to a less (v. g. calling four grains of silver a penny
to-day, when five grains of silver made a penny yesterday), but
adds no worth or real value to the silver coin, to make amends
for its want of silver. That is impossible to be done. For it is
only the quantity of silver in it that is, and eternally will be,
the measure of its value. One may as rationally hope to
lengthen a foot, by dividing it into fifteen parts instead of
twelve and calling them inches, as to increase the value of
silver that is in a shilling, by dividing it into fifteen parts instead of twelve and calling them pence. This is all that is done,
when a shilling is raised from twelve to fifteen pence."

Lowndes had maintained that "raising the coin," in
addition to making up the loss caused by calling in the
clipped money, and other advantages, would increase the
circulating medium of the country, and so put a stop to
the multiplication of hazardous paper-credit and the in-

conveniences of bartering.   Nothing could be better than
Locke's reply :—

> "Just as the boy cut his leather into five quarters (as he
> called them) to cover his ball, when cut into four quarters it
> fell short, but, after all his pains, as much of his ball lay bare
> as before ; if the quantity of coined silver, employed in Eng-
> land, fall short, the arbitrary denomination of a greater number
> of pence given to it, or, which is all one, to the several coined
> pieces of it, will not make it commensurate to the size of our
> trade or the greatness of our occasions.   This is as certain as
> that, if the quantity of a board, which is to stop a leak of a
> ship fifteen inches square, be but twelve inches square, it will
> not be made to do it by being measured by a foot that is divided
> into fifteen inches, instead of twelve, and so having a larger
> tale or number of inches in denomination given to it."

The general principle that to depreciate the coinage is
to rob the creditor, and that, though you may change the
name, you cannot change the thing, was quite as emphatically stated by Petty and North as by Locke.   But the
value of Locke's tracts consisted in their amplitude of
argument and illustration, which left to the unprejudiced
reader no alternative but to accept their conclusion.   As
he himself said in a letter to Molyneux, "Lay by the
arbitrary names of pence and shillings, and consider and
speak of it as grains and ounces of silver, and 'tis as easy
as telling of twenty."

Locke had the penetration to see that the laws existing
in his time against the exportation of gold and silver coin
must necessarily be futile, and, while it was permitted to
export bullion, could answer no conceivable purpose.
These laws, which date from the time of Edward the
Third, were, curiously enough, not repealed till the year
1819, though, as early as the time of the Restoration, they

had been pronounced by so competent a judge as Sir William Petty to be "nugatory" and "impracticable." Nothing, as Locke says towards the conclusion of his answer to Lowndes, could prevent the exportation of silver and gold in payment of debts contracted beyond the seas, and it could "be no odds to England whether it was carried out in specie or when melted down into bullion." But the principle on which the prohibition of exporting gold and silver coin ultimately rested seems to have been accepted by him as unhesitatingly as it was by almost all the other economists of the time. That principle was that the wealth of a nation is to be measured by the amount of gold and silver in its possession, this amount depending on the ratio of the value of the exports to that of the imports. When the value of the exports exceeded that of the imports, the Balance of Trade, as it was called, was said to be in favour of a country ; when, on the other hand, the value of the imports exceeded that of the exports, the Balance of Trade was said to be against it. A favourable balance, it was assumed, must necessarily increase the amount of gold and silver in the country, while an unfavourable balance must necessarily diminish it. And, lastly, the amount of gold and silver in its possession was the measure of a nation's wealth. These views form part of what political economists call the Mercantile Theory, which it was the peculiar glory of Adam Smith to demolish.

It is somewhat humiliating to the biographer of Locke to be obliged to confess that, in this respect, his theories on trade lag considerably behind those of an almost contemporary writer, Sir Dudley North, whose work has already been mentioned. Some of North's maxims are worthy of Adam Smith, and one wonders that, when once ennunciated, they found so little currency, and were so completely ignored in both the literature and the legislation of the time. Here are a few, but the whole tract may be read in less than an hour. "The whole world, as to trade, is but as one nation or people, and therein nations are as persons." "The loss of a trade with one nation is not that only, separately considered, but so much of the trade of the world rescinded and lost, for all is combined together." "No laws can set prices in trade, the rates of which must and will make themselves; but, when such laws do happen to lay any hold, it is so much impediment to trade, and therefore prejudicial." "No man is richer for having his estate all in money, plate, &c., lying by him, but, on the contrary, he is for that reason the poorer. That man is richest, whose estate is in a growing condition, either in land at farm, money at interest, or goods in trade." "Money exported in trade is an increase to the wealth of the nation; but spent in war and payments abroad, is so much impoverishment." "We may labour to hedge in the Cuckoo, but in vain; for no people ever yet grew rich by policies, but it is peace, industry, and freedom that brings trade and wealth, and nothing else."

Some of Locke's opinions on trade and finance were undoubtedly erroneous, and it must be confessed that the little tract of Sir Dudley North supplies a better summary of sound economical doctrine than any which we can find in his writings; but then this brochure is merely a summary, with little of argument or elucidation, and, perhaps, it would be difficult to point to any previous or contemporary writer, whose works are, on the whole, more important in the history of economical science than those of Locke.

o

CHAPTER XII.

To trace Locke's influence on subsequent speculation would be to write the History of Philosophy from his time to our own. In England, France, and Germany, there have been few writers on strictly philosophical questions in this century or the last who have not either quoted Locke's *Essay* with approbation or at least paid him the homage of stating their grounds for dissenting from it. In the last century, his other works, especially those on Government and Toleration, may be said to have almost formed the recognized code of liberal opinion in this country, besides exercising a considerable influence on the rapidly developing speculations which, in the middle of the century, were preparing an intellectual no less than a social revolution in France. I can here only speak of the nature of Locke's influence, and of the directions it took, in the very broadest outline, and it is the less necessary that I should enter into detail, as I have frequently adverted to it in the preceding chapters.

In England, the *Essay*, though from the first it had its ardent admirers, seemed, for some years after its appearance, to have produced its effect on English philosophical literature mainly by antagonism. Many were the critics who attacked the "new way of ideas," and attempted to show the evil consequences to morals, religion, and exact thought which must follow from the acceptance of Locke's speculations. Here and there he was defended, but the attack certainly largely outnumbered the defence. Of these controversies I have already given some account in the chapters on Locke's Life, and need not, therefore, now recur to them. The first English writer on philosophy of the highest rank who succeeded Locke was Berkeley, and on him the influence of his predecessor is so distinctly apparent, that it may well be questioned whether Berkeley would ever have written the *Principles* and the *Dialogues*, if Locke had not written the *Essay*. Locke had regarded not "things" but "ideas" as the immediate objects of the mind in thinking, though he had supposed these ideas to be representative of things; but why, argued Berkeley, suppose "things" to exist, if "ideas" are the only objects which we perceive? Again, Locke had analyzed the idea of Matter conceived as "Substance" into "we know not what" support of known qualities. How, then, said Berkeley, do we know that it exists? The idealist philosophy of Berkeley may thus be viewed as a development, on one side, of the philosophy of Locke. But Hume, by carrying Berkeley's scepticism further than he had done himself, and by questioning the reality of Substance, as applied either to matter or mind, may be said to have developed Locke's principles in a direction which was practically the very reverse of that taken by Berkeley. For the result of Berkeley's denial of "matter" was to enhance the importance of "mind," and to re-assure men as to the existence of one all-embracing mind in the person of the Deity. But the result of the questions which Hume raised as to the substantial existence of either Matter or

Mind was to leave men in a state of pure scepticism, or,
as we should now perhaps call it, Agnosticism. On the
other applications of Hume's method, I need not detain
the reader. To the ordinary common-sense Englishman,
who approached philosophical questions with interest but
without any special metaphysical aptitude, the systems
both of Hume and Berkeley appeared to be open to the
fatal objection of paradox, and, hence, throughout the
eighteenth century, Locke continued, in ordinary estimation, to hold the supreme place among English philosophers. Horace Walpole (writing in 1789) probably
expresses the average opinion of the English reading
public of his time, when he says that Locke (with whom
he couples Bacon) was almost the first philosopher who
introduced common-sense into his writings. Nor was it
only that he was supreme in popular estimation. His
influence is apparent in almost every philosophical and
quasi-philosophical work of the period. It may specially
be mentioned that the doctrine of Innate Ideas went out
of fashion, both word and thing, and, when a similar doctrine came into vogue at the end of the century, under
the authority of Reid and Stewart, it was in a modified
form and under a new appellation, that of primary or
fundamental beliefs. These authors always spoke with
the greatest respect of Locke, and Stewart especially was
always anxious to establish, when possible, an identity of
opinion between himself and his illustrious predecessor.
And even in recent times, when the topics and conditions of
philosophical speculation have undergone so much change,
there are few philosophical authors of eminence who
do not make frequent reference to Locke's *Essay*. It is
now perhaps seldom read through except by professed
students of philosophy, but it is still probably oftener

"dipped into" than any other philosophical treatise in
the language.

In France, the *Essay* at first made little way.   It took
more than twenty years to sell off the first edition of the
French translation, but from 1723 to 1758 editions
followed one another in rapid succession at intervals of
about six years.   Voltaire says that no man had been less
read or more abused in France than Locke.   The points
in his philosophy which seem to have been specially
selected for attack were the statements that God might, if
he pleased, annex thought to matter, and that the natural
reason could not alone assure us of the immortality of the
soul.   The qualifications, as the custom is, were dropped
out of these statements, and it was roundly asserted that
Locke maintained the soul to be material and mortal.
Voltaire does not fail to point out the hastiness and
injustice of these conclusions, and is himself unbounded
in his admiration for the English philosopher.   Malebranche, he says, is read on account of the agreeableness
of his style, Descartes on account of the hardihood of his
speculations ; Locke is not read, because he is merely
wise.   There never was a thinker more wise, more
methodical, more logical than Locke.   Other reasoners
had written a romance of the soul ; Locke came and
modestly wrote its history, developing the ideas of the
human understanding as an accomplished anatomist ex-
plains the forces of the human body.   Voltaire lived to
see the philosophy of Locke, or rather an extreme phase of
it, become almost the established creed of those who cared
at all for speculative questions in France.   Condillac in
his early work, the *Essai sur l'Origine des Connoissances
Humaines* (first published in 1746), simply adopts Locke's
account of the origin of knowledge, finding it in the two

sources of Sensation and Reflection. But in his later
work, the *Traité des Sensations*, which appeared in 1754,
he has gone far beyond his master, and not only finds the
origin of all knowledge in sensation alone, but of all our
faculties as well. It is in this work that the metaphor of
the gradually animated statue occurs. Condillac's system
soon became the fashionable philosophy of his countrymen, and both friends and foes credited Locke with its
parentage. With Joseph de Maistre, who may be regarded
as the bitterest exponent of French Ultramontanism, Locke
is the intermediate link through whom Helvétius, Cabanis,
and the other enemies of the human race in France had
derived from Bacon the principles which had been so
destructive to their country and mankind. But it was
not the followers of Condillac only who professed to base
their systems on the principles of Locke. Degerando,
writing in 1813, says "all the French philosophers of
this age glory in ranging themselves among the disciples
of Locke, and admitting his principles." The great
names of Turgot, Diderot, D'Alembert, Condorcet, and
Destutt de Tracy alike appear in the roll of his professed
disciples. And even when the reaction against the authority of Locke began in France, his influence might still be
traced in authors like Maine de Biran, Royer Collard,
Cousin, and Jouffroy, however emphatically they might
repudiate his system as a whole. Lastly, Auguste Comte
may be connected with Locke through Hume.

Except by way of reaction and opposition, Locke's
influence has been felt much less in Germany than in
either England or France. The earliest opponent of his
philosophy, who himself held any high rank as a philosopher, was Leibnitz, who, in his *Nouveaux Essais* (written
in 1704, but not published till 1765), attacked not only

Locke's specific conclusions but his method of commencing
the study of philosophy with an examination of the human
mind.   Yet he recognizes the *Essay* as " one of the most
beautiful and most esteemed works of this time." It may
be remarked as curious that he is disposed to rate the
Thoughts on Education even still higher than the   *ssay.*
But, when we think of Locke's relation to German philosophy, it is mainly in connexion with the antagonism of
Kant. For, though Kant states that he was " awoke from
his dogmatic slumber" by reading Hume, it is plain,
throughout the *Kritik*, that he has in his mind the system of Locke at least as much as that of his sceptical
successor.   And yet these two great philosophers, the
reformer of English and the reformer of German philosophy, have much in common, specially their mode of
approaching the problems of ontology and theology, which
have vexed so many generations of thinkers, by first
inquiring into the limits, capacities, and procedure of
the human mind.

Of the specific influence of Locke's treatises on Government, Religion, Toleration, Education, and Finance, I
have already said something in previous chapters.   In
each one of these subjects, the publication of his views
forms a point of departure, and no writer on the history
of any one of them could dispense with a lengthened
notice of his theories.

But far more important than their specific influence on
other writers, or even on the development of the subjects
with which they deal, has been the effect of Locke's
writings on the history of progress and civilization.   In
an age of excitement and prejudice, he set men the
example of thinking calmly and clearly. When philosophy was almost synonymous with the arid discussion of

scholastic subtleties, he wrote so as to interest statesmen
and men of the world. At a time when the chains of
dogma were far tighter, and the penalties of attempting to
loosen them far more stringent, than it is now easy to
conceive, he raised questions which stirred the very depths
of human thought. And all this he did in a spirit so
candid, so tolerant, so liberal, and so unselfish, that he
seemed to be writing not for his own party or his own
times but for the future of knowledge and of mankind.
To sound every question to the bottom, never to allow our
convictions to outstrip our evidence, to throw aside all
prejudices and all interests in the pursuit of truth, but to
hold the truth, when found, in all charity and with all
consideration towards those who have been less fortunate
than we—these are the lessons which, faithfully transmitted through two centuries by those who had eyes to
see and ears to hear, he has bequeathed to us and our
posterity.

GILBERT AND RIVINGTON, PRINTERS, ST. JOHN'S SQUARE, LONDON.

For EU product safety concerns, contact us at Calle de José Abascal, 56–1°, 28003 Madrid, Spain or eugpsr@cambridge.org.